Rising Out

✴

CLASSICS OF IRISH HISTORY
General Editor: Tom Garvin

Original publication dates of reprinted titles are given in brackets

Rising Out

Seán Connolly of Longford
(1890–1921)

✶

ERNIE O'MALLEY

edited by Cormac K. H. O'Malley

UNIVERSITY COLLEGE DUBLIN PRESS
Preas Choláiste Ollscoile Bhaile Átha Cliath

First published in 2007 by
University College Dublin Press
© Cormac K. H. O'Malley 2007

ISBN 978-1-904558-89-7
ISSN 1393-6883

University College Dublin Press
Newman House, 86 St Stephen's Green
Dublin 2, Ireland
www.ucdpress.ie

Cataloguing in Publication data available from
the British Library

Typeset in Ireland in Ehrhardt by Elaine Burberry
Text design by Lyn Davies, Frome, Somerset, England
Printed in England on acid-free paper
by Athenæum Press, Gateshead

CONTENTS

ABBREVIATIONS

Adj.	Adjutant
Batt.	Battalion
Bde	Brigade
BMH	Bureau of Military History
EOM	Ernie O'Malley
GHQ	General Headquarters
HQ	Headquarters
IO	Information Officer
IRA	Irish Republican Army
IRB	Irish Republican Brotherhood
O/C	Officer Commanding
QM	Quartermaster
RIC	Royal Irish Constabulary
UCDA	University College Dublin Archives
VOC	Vice-Commandant

INTRODUCTION

Cormac K. H. O'Malley

This memoir records part of the story of Seán Connolly, one of the many minimally documented nationalist activists, who gave their lives for the cause of Irish freedom in the War of Independence, 1919–21. Connolly came from Ballinalee, Co. Longford and was nurtured in a tradition of Irish nationalism through cultural connections in local musical activities, his football prowess in the Gaelic Athletic Association, and his family knowledge of local history. He joined the Irish Volunteers, the Irish Republican Brotherhood, the Irish Republican Army and participated in military activities in Longford, Roscommon and finally Leitrim, where he was fatally wounded at the battle of Selton Hill on 11 March 1921. His story is told in greater detail in this memoir by my father, Ernie O'Malley, where it is placed in the historical perspective of other events which were occurring locally and nationally at that time. However, in this introduction I want to relate how this memoir came into existence and was published as well as providing a brief description of my father's own role in that period of Irish history. Though I presume my father never actually met Seán Connolly, this memoir relates how their lives were interconnected, and it is and for that reason, I think, that he inserts himself as an active participant in several chapters of this memoir.[1]

GENESIS OF SEÁN CONNOLLY MANUSCRIPT

My father wrote his own account of his involvement in national and military activities from 1916 to 1924 while he was in America in the 1930s, far removed from any records of the actual events. His account, as published in London and Dublin in 1936 in *On Another Man's Wound*,[2] gives an overview of how Irish nationalism led to effective military action in the early twentieth century, but he published only the first half of his story and stopped at the Truce as of 12 July 1921. He was advised that publishing a more detailed analysis of the post-Truce disintegration of Irish political and military affairs might prove inadvisable in terms of libel actions. As it was, he was sued for libel on the less controversial first half of his story. That event had a dampening effect on any other historical writing for some years.

During the early 1940s father recommenced his work on his earlier unpublished manuscript on the military events subsequent to the Truce up through the Civil War. He found that his life as a farmer in Co. Mayo did not allow him time to do the necessary research on the facts in order to make the story accurate for purposes of publication, and the manuscript was once again shelved. He did subsequently work on it, and it was eventually published posthumously as *The Singing Flame* in 1979.[3]

In the mid-1940s, a movement was afoot to create a government-sponsored institution that would record the history of the earlier struggle for independence.[4] Opinion was divided as to when such a reservoir of memoirs should start and end. Father was in touch with some of the personalities who were shaping that debate about the institution, including Florence O'Donoghue. In fact, he wanted to obtain certain military information from Florrie. A Bureau of Military History was eventually created, with the objective of preserving history from 1913 until the Truce, thus leaving out activities during the Truce, the Treaty negotiations and the Civil War.

Since father had been against the Treaty and was ultimately appointed Assistant Chief of Staff to Liam Lynch, the Chief of Staff of the Anti-Treaty Republicans, he felt strongly that any recording of history should also document the events of those years. The Bureau proceeded to advertise and ask for survivors to come forward to make their statements to the Bureau staff. Over a ten-year period 1,773 survivors submitted information, some long, some short and some with supplemental documentation. These typed records were not available to the public until 2005.[5] Father had set about gathering information between 1948 and 1954. He interviewed over 450 men and women, only 130 of whom had given statements to the Bureau. He felt that his own system of personal interview, during which he took handwritten notes, and perhaps carried out some cross-examination on his own, would allow him – and thus others – to get at the truth when there appeared to be conflicting positions on a particular incident. In many cases he went back for a second and third interview, and sometimes he held group interviews. Father felt that he could obtain enough information in this manner to provide thorough documentation for recollections of a largely Republican group, as well as to allow him to confirm his own Civil War autobiography. Most of the 320 survivors who did not give their statements to the Bureau were Anti-Treaty Republicans. Once he had written up his initial interview in a First Series of notebooks, he then rewrote the entire interview in more legible handwriting in his Second Series. All of these Military Notebooks were presented to University College Dublin Archives in 1974 and have been available to the general public for research since then.[6]

In the course of the interviews, father would have noticed the common theme of how local brigades were organised and how their activities were usually dependent on the energies of a few outstanding local leaders. He was already well aware of this, since his own role of working for three years under Michael Collins and Richard Mulcahy from 1918 to late 1920 had been to 'organise' or 'reorganise' the local Irish Volunteer brigades so that they would be stimulated to take military action. The strategy for the master plan to counter and remove British political and military presence in Ireland required local military actions throughout the country, apart from other non-military activities. These were aimed both at defeating the Royal Irish Constabulary, the Auxiliaries and the Black and Tans and at gaining the confidence and loyalty of the local people. In fulfilling his mission to a brigade area, father would help to select and appoint local officers, then train them and their men, and move on after a few weeks.

When father came to write up the interviews some thirty years later, he was struck by the fact that history had overlooked so many local leaders. Near the beginning of the present memoir, he notes:

> It might be difficult for most people to answer from what districts the following men came: Mick Fitzgerald, Seán Wall, Martin Devitt, Paddy Ryan Lacken, Seamus Devins, Jerry Kiely, Thomas Traynor, Tom Keogh, and Seán Connolly. We have no speeches from the dock to illustrate their lives at a critical moment. In their time a prisoner was tried in secret before a group of officers. The only record that the public heard of was their sentence, or if they died in action, or through treachery, their own district holds threads of their weaving. The last mentioned name, Seán Connolly, has been forgotten, and maybe some of his story can be made into a patchwork quilt from memory.[7]

While father made his way around Ireland interviewing in the early 1950s, he visited the counties of Longford, Leitrim and Roscommon. He had been involved there in earlier years in organising brigade structures, and was therefore familiar with some of the survivors. During his interviews in those counties, he encountered the story of Seán Connolly and decided to tell it, but the story's journey to publication has been long and tortuous.

At the time that my father's papers were being prepared to establish the Ernie O'Malley Archives at University College Dublin in the early 1970s, I was aware that the Seán Connolly manuscript existed, but many events delayed its publication. My first efforts had been to find a publisher for a previously published book, *On Another Man's Wound*, rather than for an unpublished manuscript. Anvil Books republished it in 1978, after several other Irish publishers had declined to do so. Then came in succession publication by Anvil of *The Singing Flame* and *Raids and Rallies*.[8] With the help and devotion of Frances-Mary Blake as editor, both of these manuscripts were published. *Raids and Rallies* had been previously published as a long-running series in the *Sunday Press* in 1955–6.

In 1984 Padraic O'Farrell published a short biography, *The Ernie O'Malley Story*.[9] In 1991, Richard English and I co-edited *Prisoners: The Civil War Letters of Ernie O'Malley*,[10] which was followed in 1996 by his full biography, *Ernie O'Malley: IRA Intellectual*.[11]

In 2002 I started to expand *Prisoners* from 48 letters to 400 letters and this required considerable research through many archives with significant work by my co-editor Anne Dolan.[12] Finally, in 2004, I started to consider the Connolly manuscript. After many discussions, it was thought that publishing the manuscript as originally written with a brief introduction would be best. With that thought in mind, I approached University College Dublin Press, and they agreed that the short biographical memoir would fit well into their reprint series.

Once the publisher was lined up, I then began to edit father's original typed manuscript. I should add that I have never found the original handwritten manuscript, but the typed version had been edited by him. With the unstinting help of several supporters, I conformed the spellings of names and places, made punctuation changes, added first names where they could be found, added notes to give further background, included a brief biographical sketch on the principal local participants, prepared a detailed index, located appropriate illustrations, but overall made the minimum possible changes to the original text.

As early as 1984 I received a letter from Seán Connolly's nephew, Donal MacLochlainn of Lifford, Co. Donegal, enquiring whether there was any truth in a rumour he had heard that a draft biography existed. I replied positively, but said it would be pursued at some time in the future. Donal's mother, Maura, was Seán Connolly's younger sister, and as a teenager had been able to play a most helpful role as courier for communications, arms and ammunition to Dublin and around the county. She, like many of the official or unofficial members of Cumman na mBan, played a significant role in facilitating what the IRA accomplished. In late 2006, I found my 1984 letter to Donal, and in a moment I phoned him. There we were, talking about his uncle, my father and local Longford history. Well, that was an inspiration, and urged me on to make sure the project got completed this time.

One of the challenges in editing a book about a person for whom there is little collateral evidence in the standard historical tomes is that it is hard to secure confirmatory information. However, I was aware that my father had interviewed over twenty of the survivors of the Seán Connolly story between 1950 and 1952, and that therefore he had had a sound basis for his final version of the facts. These interviews included in Longford: Séamus Conway, Frank Davis, Pat McGrath, Maura Connolly [MacLochlainn], Pat

Mulleray, and Mick Murphy; in Roscommon: Frank Davis, Bill Doherty, Luke Duffy, Martin Fallon, Jim Feely, John Kelly, Pat Mullolly, Tom O'Reilly, Dan O'Rourke, Seán Owens, and Frank Simmons; and in Leitrim: Charlie and Jim Flynn, Frank MacKeown, Paddy Morrissey, and Paddy Mulleray. I also discovered correspondence from other people to my father about Connolly as well as his exchanges with James J. Brady, formerly of Longford, who was then living in New York City.

Support for preparing this manuscript for publication has come from many sources, and together we have made a team effort. Ed Ginty of New York introduced me to the Longford County Historical Society, and there I found unstinting assistance from James MacNerney and Martin Morris, the Archivist for Longford County Council, and translation assistance from Joe Hunt. They in turn received support for local facts and dates from Sr Maeve Brady, Mary Dodd, Jimmy Lennon, Noel Heslin, Sean Lynch, the Mick Murphy family, Tommy Nevin, Jonathan Walsh and the *Longford Leader* (microfilm in Longford Library and Archives). Donal MacLochlainn gave me all he could about his uncle Seán Connolly. Dr Eileen Reilly, who was born in Ballinalee and knew from childhood the stories of Seán Connolly, happened to be Acting Director of Glucksman Ireland House at New York University, where I had been on the Board of Advisers for over eight years. Cormac Ó Suilleabhain has been most helpful regarding Leitrim matters as has Katherine Hegarty Thorne whose book on Roscommon was published in 2005.[13] My thanks also to the Commanding Officer, Connolly Barracks, Longford, for permission to reproduce the image of Seán Connolly. John O'Callaghan at University of Limerick was also most helpful. To them, to many others and particularly to my family for giving me support and understanding for this effort, I am deeply indebted.

ERNIE O'MALLEY

Father was born in Castlebar, Co. Mayo, the second of eleven children. His parents moved to Dublin in 1906 where his father became a clerk in the Congested Districts Board, a nice, secure, low-level administrative functionary post. Unlike his older brother Frank who joined the Royal Dublin Fusiliers in 1914 upon completion of secondary school, father was fortunate to win a Dublin City Scholarship to study medicine at University College Dublin in 1915. He was thus in Dublin when the counter-countermanded Rising occurred on Easter Monday 1916. The events which he experienced during those few days were to change his life and served as his epiphany. He finally understood why the Fenians and their forebears had been saying that Ireland should be for the Irish and that the physical force struggle to achieve that objective was necessary and worthy of sacrifice.

While he remained at the Cecilia Street medical campus of UCD, his heart and mind were elsewhere, and he could not concentrate on his medical studies. Having joined up with the newly reactivated Irish Volunteers in 1917, by early 1918 he decided to leave home and go on the run. His assignments for the next almost three years were to 'organise' local brigades to which he was sent by Michael Collins and Richard Mulcahy. He always made copious notes on conditions, volunteer staff levels and supplies so that he could report in detail on the local events to headquarters. He became known as a 'man of action'. In 1917 he walked into Dublin Castle in his brother's British officer's uniform and asked for and received a pistol and ammunition for his 'protection' on the unruly streets of Dublin. He would regularly lead his troops into action be it on the rooftop when assaulting a barracks of the Royal Irish Constabulary or in an ambush on Auxiliary troops.

During one of his organising expeditions in Kilkenny in December 1920, he was arrested and gave his name as Bernard Stewart. He was transferred to Dublin Castle where even the notorious Major King and Captain J. L. Hardy could not persuade him with red hot pokers and a pistol using blanks to disclose any other information. In an incident at their Christmas dinner he refused to drink the health of the king, since he explained simply that the king was not *his* king. He was fortunate that when transferred to the infamous Kilmainham Jail, he was able to escape – one of only four men ever to do so in its long nefarious history. Once free, he took up his assignment as Commandant-General in charge of the 2nd Southern Division, then a martial law area covering East Limerick, Tipperary, and parts of Carlow and Kilkenny. Liam Lynch was in charge of the 1st Southern Division. He was incredulous when the Truce was declared in July 1921, but took advantage of the peace to train and illegally arm his troops in order to be ready for the inevitable resumption since England had not yet agreed to Irish freedom.

When he heard the news that the Treaty had been signed, he was furious. He wrote to Eamon de Valera, then President of the Dáil Éireann and effectively the Irish Republic, and pledged to him, as President, allegiance of the fighting troops of the 1st, 2nd and 3rd Southern Divisions. However, during the debates on the Treaty, when de Valera submitted his Document Number Two, which did not refer to the recognition of an Irish Republic, father withdrew his support for de Valera. From then on even before the end of December 1921, he – and many other hardline republicans – felt that a line had been drawn. Though appointed to some posts to help monitor and bridge the developing rift between the two camps in the formerly united IRA Headquarters Staff, he refused to participate. Instead, he was in Limerick in March and almost precipitated the Civil War when he demanded that Limerick be handed over to him from the evacuating British army troops rather than the Free State Army, since Limerick was located within his 2nd Southern Division. In the end the Free State Army withdrew peacefully. He was then appointed Director of Organisation for the Anti-Treaty Republicans and proceeded to attempt to build up an effective fighting force should such be required. He moved his office to the Four Courts in Dublin when those buildings were taken over by the Republicans in April. Subsequently, when the buildings came under attack by the Free State troops on 28 June, though he was junior in rank to others, he was asked to take charge of the defence of the Four Courts. When it was time for a surrender of the blazing buildings, he opposed it but was ordered to do so, and, in deep humiliation, he marched the surviving troops out for the surrender.

In the chaos which occurred immediately after the surrender and the detention of the Republicans in Jameson's Distillery, father managed to escape once again with a small cadre of officers. Within days he took charge of the command vacuum and led a counter attack on the Free State Army in several counties in Leinster. Soon thereafter Liam Lynch appointed him – at age 25 – as Acting Assistant Chief of Staff with responsibility for the Ulster and Leinster Divisions, while Lynch retained Connaught and Munster. For four months he directed a fairly ineffective campaign against the more heavily armed and established Free State National Army. He was not sorry when Michael Collins was killed. Eventually, he himself was captured and almost killed in November 1922.

During father's jail-time experience from November 1922 to July 1924, he tried to recover his health, but his wounds had been severe and conditions were poor. Had he recovered his health sufficiently to stand trial, he would have been court-martialled, as the charges had already been served on him and he would not have denied them. The outcome would probably have been inevitable. During his slow recovery in jail, he was elected a member of the

Dáil for North Dublin in August 1923, but he would never take his seat on principle even when out of jail. In October 1923, he joined with many others in a 41-day hunger strike which was called off only when one of his comrades died. He would have been willing to continue for the cause, but did not.

While in jail, much of his time was spent in satisfying his voracious appetite for reading books on art, literature, poetry and languages. He set himself, in effect, a university reading course in several fields and sought advice from experts on the outside to direct his reading. His extensive letters to Mrs Erskine Childers, published in *Prisoners*,[14] mentioned the subjects that interested him. In the end, however, he indicated that he would not pursue the struggle and when he left jail in 1924 he went off to Europe to recover his health.

SYMBOLISM OF SEÁN CONNOLLY

One could read a degree of bitterness and irony into the title of father's best-known work as it is based on an Ulster proverb 'it's easy to sleep on another man's wound'. Father was not ultimately embittered against the English or the Free Staters against whom he fought. He effectively dropped out of the military and political arena and preferred to savour the artistic and literary contacts which he subsequently pursued. He made a name for himself as an art critic, essayist, folklorist, and latterly as military historian. While pursuing this softer side of life, he appreciated more and more that the truth had eventually to be told about what had occurred in the struggle for Irish independence from 1912 to 1924.

One of the key elements in that period of struggle, as I see it, was the role played by the small local leaders. In the course of his 450 interviews in 25 of the 32 counties of Ireland, he saw many examples of how critical and effective those local leaders were to the cause. No doubt he was mindful of the fact that he had himself been one of those local leaders, providing stimulus and energy by example to the communities he visited. I think he must have felt that the difference between the eventual success of the IRA military efforts during the War of Independence and all the other unsuccessful attempts at insurrection in Ireland's turbulent history had been the key role played by the local organisers. There had always been headquarters people with great names and lofty general plans, but only at this time was effective concerted effort on the ground carried out by local men in their local areas: men like Seán Connolly, who if they were killed in action were rarely heard of again. In father's own case, he had done the organising as well as holding higher command, but that was rare. Thus the tale of Seán Connolly as related by my father is a tribute to the efforts of men like Seán Connolly all around Ireland. Though Connolly met with many failures in his years of struggle, he never lost faith, never gave up and always continued on target.

Rising Out

✦

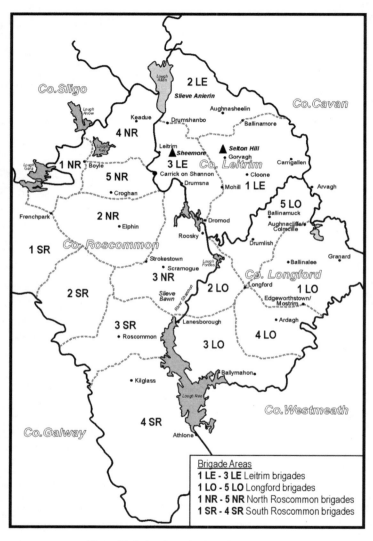

Map of Leitrim, Longford and Roscommon
Map drawn by Stephen Hannon

Chapter 1

Longford

Once upon a time within our own memories, a stranger could find in many a house in a remote mountain, or on a wide tract of bogland, a number of well-worn books. A few of them would have paper covers, but others would show a cloth back. They were: *Antrim and Down in '98*, *The History of Ireland* by John Mitchel, *Jail Journal* or *Five Years in British Prisons*, *New Ireland*, *Speeches from the Dock*.[1] I have listened to old men who could recite parts of these books, especially the speeches made by men who were expecting death or life imprisonment. I can remember an old Clare man near Doolin, who had built his house with the aid of a round shot with which he had broken up scattered limestone boulders as he raised the walls. A gunboat had been wrecked on the near coast, and he had used its contribution to help in making his home. While he showed me the round shot, he held up his hand peremptorily as if the silence the neighbourhood while he rolled forth:

The year of grace 1867, dawned upon a cloudy and troublous period in Irish politics. Danger was brewing throughout the land; under the crust of society the long confined larva of Fenianism effervesced and glowed. Strange rumours filled the air; strange sounds were heard at night on the hill-sides and in the meadows; and, through the dim moonlight, masses of men were seen in secluded spots moving in regular bodies and practising military evolutions. From castle and mansion and country seat, the spectre of alarm glided to and fro, whispering with bloodless lips of coming convulsions and slaughter, of the opening of the crater of revolution and of a war against property and class.[2]

As the old man blessed his rhetoric I listened while my thoughts were busy as well with what had happened to me that day of the year 1919, in the stony indifference of the Burren.

The old man's reiteration of the printed page was a weak addendum to his long and detailed memory of Fenianism and of the Land War of the 1880s which combined had helped to weaken the grasp of landlordism. His own vivid words and strong phrasing were at war with the garnished book words, but he at least knew the two renditions. A later generation which accepts what freedom there is has too often neither the paper-backed books nor the guidance of a retention which would emphasise or soften the immediate past.

That unrest, promoted by the physical presence of the British, which laid its heavy historical burden on former generations, was resolved as a result of the success of the War of Independence. The burden was economic, physical and mental to some, but the British straightjacket of overlordship could produce in others emotional and psychological effects, which were as constricting in their antipathy as the other results of foreign power and influence. The change in the language we spoke had also produced in the British a sense that they were dealing with a section of their own people, and so for them undertones and overtones of English spoken by the conquered met with no understanding.

The older generation among us speaks a language of its own to itself, much as a former generation spoke Irish to itself whenever they wished to say things the children were not to overhear. Its connotations make no difficulties, its allusions are quickly understood; but what unites listeners and speakers is a sense of comradeship shared in stress and difficulties, when wits and physical senses were shattered by an attempt to deal with odds hard to overcome or circumvent. In that sharing, money or influence had little value as an introduction to danger. Standards of judgments are in the main accepted by one another, on men and on events, and when men are not swayed by memory of a subsequent civil war, by politics or self-interest these judgments yet hold good.

When the mechanics of an oppression are gone the symbols of an oppression are no longer valid, yet they can be remembered in folklore and recreated in writing. Song and story that once stirred men no longer move a younger generation. The memory of a red coat made a crimson scar on the thoughts of a generation older than our own, for was it not 'England's hated red', yet we lived to see the coat as a piece of bright decoration in childhood. But we had a very different regard for a khaki uniform. The bottle green of the Royal Irish Constabulary is unknown as a menace outside of part of Ulster. In time these colours may take on a quality of other worldliness which may induce them to be regarded as fairy tales.

Some time ago in each country district there were a number of names of dead men on the lips of people, but it is exceptional now to hear these men mentioned. Even the ballads which were written about attack and ambush, or because of a sudden killing of a man, and which were sung at dances and through fairs have been forgotten. Seemingly, it takes a few drinks in company to stimulate that ballad sense by releasing a hidden sluice gate shut down by the years. Then it lapses again until in an out of the way place a tinker may strengthen an echo, or a singer at a wake may give it life again.

As a race we have not kept records, nor have we written in anything but the sparsest way about movements or organisations which have influenced us since the Land Wars. Our sources are meagre enough and when we go further back in time certain periods have to depend upon the special pleading of the State Papers rather than the unearthing of that more difficult and leavening material which

Daniel Corkery once so ably used in *The Hidden Ireland*. Only in the writing about of the events of our own times can they be revived even if it be from the tangent of bias and only when seen in print can the folklore embroidery be properly adjusted. Standish O'Grady who had a good knowledge of official records in Elizabethan times remarks:

> The State Papers make us think meanly of everyone, of the officials as well as of the chieftains. On the other hand, the magnanimity of the Four Masters includes all: Sir John Perrott, Sir Richard Bingham, and Sir Conyers Clifford move through their pages with something of the past of ancient heroes.[3]

It might be difficult for most people to answer from what districts the following men came: Mick Fitzgerald, Seán Wall, Martin Devitt , Paddy Ryan Lacken, Seamus Devins, Jerry Kiely, Thomas Traynor, Tom Keogh and Seán Connolly.[4] We have no speeches from the dock to illustrate their lives at a critical moment. In their time a prisoner was tried in secret before a group of officers. The only record that the public heard of was their sentence, or if they died in action, or through treachery – their own district holds threads of their weaving. The last mentioned name, Seán Connolly, has been forgotten, and maybe some of his story can be made into a patchwork quilt from memory.

Seán Connolly was born in France, near the village of Ballinalee, Co. Longford in 1890, and in that same year, some months afterwards, two of his later companions were also born, Pat MacGrath and Seán Duffy. There were five boys and two girls in the Connolly family.[5] His father, John Connolly, was an eggler. He wandered around the district with a horse and spring van, and as he had a small shop at his house, he could exchange groceries for eggs. When the boys grew up they went to school to his uncle Master

Michael Connolly who taught near Clonbroney Chapel. Seán MacEoin, who was their junior by a few years, was in a lower class. Seán Connolly remained at school until he reached the second sixth standard which was the highest class. He was the eldest of a growing family and his help was needed on his father's small farm, but in the winter months he went to a night school which was conducted by his uncle. The Connollys had a tradition of mastering, for Seán's grandfather, Andrew Connolly, had been the first teacher to instruct in Ballinalee.

About forty young lads attended regularly in the advanced school, but a few of them were grown lads who carried their clay pipes in their pockets or chewed on a piece of plug tobacco as a sign of manhood. Some were preparing to emigrate to North America where they, who knew only of land and the ways of the land, would join relatives and friends who had already strengthened the protection groups of their own race in the strident clash of large cities. Others made use of the night school to help them pass the examination for an entry into the ranks of the Royal Irish Constabulary or the RIC, as it was known. Their background had to be innocent of rebel upbringing or tradition, which might in any way influence their future loyalty. They would have to be sanctioned by the sergeant and by the nearest head constable. Then they interviewed the District Inspector and the County Inspector, before they were safe to approach the Depot in the Phoenix Park, Dublin.[6] There in Master Connolly's winter classes sat boys who were close enough to each other in their way of life, but who would later take sides which drifted further and further apart until a deep chasm separated those who were in the IRA from their schoolfellows in the RIC.

An old music teacher, Francis McDonagh of Kilshrewley, taught the fiddle as he moved around from parish to parish. Bernard Rodgers, a famous teacher who had taught in Esker school, had been a pupil of Tom Kiernan who was blind. He had been taught, it is said, by Turlough O'Carolan, but as the blind composer died in 1738 the gap in time seems too large for two teachers to fill. The music teacher might remain in a district for close on a month. He would give lessons to the boys of the house in which he stayed in exchange for his care and keep, but his other pupils would pay for their instruction. Traditional music and song were mingled with dances to round off the teacher's knowledge of jigs, sets and reels. His company was a social event as well, among people who seldom travelled beyond their market town except to a fair. He was a link between parishes in their own and in other counties. The teacher had a knowledge of current movements and events. He was listened to with great respect by the people among whom he moved, and he knew how to win favour by his particular blend of gossip, courtesy and desire to please. He had pride in his professional knowledge, and his expected coming was eagerly looked forward to. He livened the evening while he passed on his repertoire of music and of talk. Like a moving snowball he gathered the honey of local extravagant doings and sayings; for the elders he had gossip which made them shake the bogdeal rafters when the youngsters were in bed. His auxiliary in the life of the neighbourhood was the good storyteller who kept a circle of listeners amused and interested by his awareness of poetry, and of baroque prose.

The 1798 background was passed over lightly around Ballinalee. The young lads seemed to know of '98, the year of the French, through song rather than through traditional memory. Although the French had spent only two days as a fighting force in Longford, the British had helped to preserve their passage by a generous use of rope. In Ballinalee over 140 Irishmen were hanged. The Croppy Field near the village was a quiet witness to those who had paid their tribute. There had been an attack on Granard by the United Irishmen, who had hoped to be able to capture the town and then hold it until the French would reach them. It was hoped that

Granard could be used as a base to gather in the United Irishmen from the midlands, but the attack was defeated.

The 1898 centenary had witnessed many monuments to the men who had died and it had revived old stories. The Irish Republican Brotherhood or IRB made use of the gatherings and the speeches to recruit more men. The Land War in Ballinalee and the neighbourhood[7] was another fighting episode which could gain colour in the telling. In Ballinamuck when the French had surrendered on terms for themselves, the police barracks was a strongly built post with rounded corner towers to give it castellated strength. Perhaps its menacing rifle slits were a tribute to '98 and the Land War. The British had a habit of preparing for the next rising by building strongholds where there had been any fighting in a previous attempt.

The country around Ballinalee had land which was fair to middling. The average holding was from twelve to twenty acres, but there was a creamery in Ballinalee and two others within a radius of three miles. The lads were needed on farms until such time as they grew up. Seán Connolly spent his time on the land. He had an interest in machinery. He could take his mother's sewing machine to pieces and assemble it, and he could take down farm machinery and repair damaged parts. He often wished that he could become an engineer but in his time there was no county council scholarships to help on ambition for the reason that there was no university then except Trinity College. The entrance to Trinity by way of scholarship was through accredited schools, which were mainly grammar schools. In the Tan War this dabbling of his in mechanics was converted to an interest in weapons, mines and explosives.

The Wilsons of Currygrane had owned the Connolly holding until a land act had broken up their estate. Currygrane House with its encirclement of wood was about a mile across country from the small Connolly farm. Here the Wilson family had grown up. Their names are yet remembered locally: Arthur, Cecil, Jimmy and Henry. Henry's name has had a larger circulation, for it was he who reorganised the Military Staff College, became a friend of General Ferdinand Foch before the war, and had finally been made Chief of the Imperial General Staff. He was to become the chief Orange watchdog among the Tories in army and governmental circles. He, a soldier, was able to advise other soldiers about mutiny. Sir John French had decided in 1913 that he would obey the King's orders if instructed to move on Ulster, but Henry Wilson told him that he himself 'would not fire on the North at the dictation of John Redmond, and this is what the whole thing means'. Later that year it was agreed that Ulster would be given belligerent rights if she resisted the British troops by force. Wilson was the British military adviser during the Tan War, and the intimate ally of the Six County police. Around Ballinalee and radiating in all directions towards Granard, Rathmore and Drumlish, there were strong pockets of armed and unarmed Orangemen, some of whom took an active part occasionally when the fight developed.

The Wilsons owned the shooting and game rights of their former properties, and they bought up further game areas. Seán Connolly and his friend Pat MacGrath fished for trout in the Camlin River and for pike and perch in Gorteen and Currygrane Lakes. Gamekeepers had to be avoided as they fished, but especially when they used a shot gun on pheasants and duck or snares on rabbits. The gamekeepers came to MacGrath's public house to drink, and when they were within was the time for the two boys to be without. Connolly was as useful at preparing a fishing tackle as he was at thatching a roof or in repairing old shot guns. The ground and water they shot over or fished in made them alert. It gave them an eye for detail, movement and colour, which made instinctive scouts of them, and the intimate knowledge of ground made scouts of other lads throughout the county.

Seán and Pat would turn up at a country dance to play polkas, quadrilles, mazurkas and that more difficult set, the Alberts. Many a house had a fiddle on the wall, or a flute, a melodeon or a concertina. Any night in the long evenings when there were five or six lads together one of them would take down a fiddle or melodeon and, if a song was asked for, the group would join in the chorus. People made their own amusement then through song, dance or instrument. Seán was a good whistler and his distinctive whistle could be recognised at a distance as he shaped his mouth to a stray memory of songs and airs.

His fiddle he played with zeal and affection by himself or in company with Pat MacGrath in whose house the boys had been taught the use of the instrument. Both of them joined the local band which was trained by O'Connell, a bandmaster who had served with and had taught in the British army. To this collection of 37 pieces the two friends contributed their share on the 'F' flutes. Band instruments were dear and money was very scarce then, but the money was raised in many ways. As time passed the band itself became disturbed, and the disturbance spread from kettle drum to buglers. Many of the members belonged to the Ancient Order of Hibernians, and this unrest dated from the time John Redmond, the Irish Parliamentary Party leader, had offered Irish bodies in exchange for English promises.[8]

The English promise as something to be distrusted by Irishmen was an historical allusion, believed by some, doubted by others. At the beginning of the First World War the British had promised a partial freedom in the form of the Home Rule Act but had postponed it until the war would be over. In return for this promise Irishmen for the first time in their history were spending blood freely in British armies. They could be trusted sufficiently far as to die for the freedom of many nationalities for which the British were ostensibly fighting, but they could not die for their own nation

as a political fact. In 1916 the trench dug for the executed leaders
became a wide gorge, and the blood spilt became by symbol a
torrent. Threats of conscription built barriers beyond this gorge.
Seán Connolly's mind was already made up. He would no longer
trust the Irish Parliamentary Party and when other players reached
that point of distrust the music itself was disharmonious. The
flageolet turned against the 'F' flutes, and the emphatic spit of the
trombone player challenged that of the trumpets.

The great banner, which headed processions, stretched in
front of the marching bandsmen, and was adorned with brilliant
streamers. The figure of Robert Emmet filled the forward side.
Two men carried the standards which bore the banner on high and
two men also held the bright cords at the sides. The holding of the
cords was no sinecure when a wind blew for then Robert Emmet
began to thrust himself forward and to roll sideways, flap back
suddenly against the standard bearers and it was now as difficult to
control as a lug sail in a sudden squall. Often behind such a costly
piece of poplin and paint marched the Forresters[9] in tight-fitting
faun trousers which were always more difficult to get out of than to
get into. A bright green uniform coat and a billy cocked hat with a
trembling ostrich plume completed the costume, which was said to
be based on the uniform Emmet wore when he led his few men
against Dublin Castle in 1803. It might well be the costume in a
drab age of a fairy prince who was lighting up a dark world.

The Robert Emmet banner was carried off later into captivity
by the porter bottled Tans and with him for company went three
kettle drums, a grand new big drum, and the music making instruments. It is not recorded what tunes the Tans played as they returned
from the raid, for they had a discordant sense of humour at times,
nor is it known what happened to poor Robert Emmet again in the
hands of his country's enemies, or to the 'F' flutes in particular.
Maybe they amused themselves when the drink was in by rallying

on the kettle drums and blowing heavily into the suffering brass for when drink mounts harmony can be avoided. Perhaps the pieces made their way, as did a great store of watches, rings and bracelets collected quickly in town and countryside, across the Irish Sea. Later like the 'old Orange flute', the musical instruments may have played Loyalist tunes at times in various English bands, far away from their pristine memories of 'O'Donnell Abu' and 'The Young May Moon'.

The drums were silent after 1916 not only in Ballinalee but throughout Ireland. With them, for the time being, went the rhetorical flourish of the drummer and the rhetorical mouthings of the parliamentarians. The glib windy phrase, the easy promise, the pleasant air of patronage went on holidays with the flamboyant banner. No longer would the backstairs approach and the differential thimble rigging of jobbery smooth the way, for now there was no expected reward for work done. The getting of freedom was not to be left to pleasant gentlemen in nice hats but was becoming more and more the business of the people themselves.

Chapter 2

Longford, 1916–18

There had been an Irish Volunteer organisation in Longford before 1916, but when the Irish Parliamentary Party (IPP) attempted to control the Volunteers by forcing them to accept their numerous nominees on the committee, which controlled the organisation, there had been a split in the organisation. As a result of this split, the Irish National Volunteers company in Ballinamuck, which had then two hundred Volunteers, no longer acted as a Volunteer company. It had been trained by British army reservists who quickly rejoined their regiments when the European war commenced.

There had been a fresh incentive to recruit the Irish Volunteers, when some of the prisoners who had been arrested after Easter Week had been released from internment camps. As a result, many young men joined Sinn Féin clubs or became members of Volunteer companies, which met in secret. In April 1917, Joseph McGuinness, then a prisoner in Lewes Prison, was selected as a parliamentary candidate for the constituency of South Longford.[1] The prisoner had not first been consulted as to whether he was willing to stand or not. Word of his selection had been smuggled into the jail by means of the underground method of communication.

Eamon de Valera was then in charge of the prisoners at Lewes, and as a result of better organisation amongst the prisoners conditions had been slightly improved. They were now allowed to talk while they were at exercise although they were otherwise treated as convicts. And talk they did when the news came in, for many of the prisoners including de Valera and McGuinness himself were hostile to the procedure of using the machinery of the British government to fight the election. The result of the numerous talks in the prison yard was that the prisoners refused to accept their fellow convict as a candidate and the fellow convict thoroughly agreed with their decision, but the men outside were determined that McGuinness would be a candidate whether he was willing or not.

The selection of a convict as a candidate was a definite challenge to the British government as it was a defiance to the Irish Parliamentary Party. Longford was a strong and well organised IPP seat, and although the Nationalist politicians were amused at this invasion of their firm position, they at once set their now powerful machine to work. Roscommon had upset the traditional Nationalists when Count George Noble Plunkett had been returned in February 1917. The candidate was a well-known and learned man. His son, Joseph, had been executed by the British in 1916 and his two other sons, Seoirse and Eoin, had been sentenced to death and, being reprieved, were then convicts. Joe McGuinness who had come from close to Tarmonbarry on the Roscommon side of the Shannon was not known to many in the Longford constituency, but his brother, Frank McGuinness, who had a shop in Longford town, was better known. McGuinness was both a symbol and a challenge, and as a challenge the Irish Parliamentary Party decided to defeat this now definite attempt to confront them with a man who had fought in Easter Week. Before this election the candidate's election representative had stated that McGuinness would not, if elected, go to the House of Commons as a member. Count Plunkett's victory in North Roscommon had come as a surprise victory; now here was a cold-blooded opposition to the IPP policy of Irish representation in the British House of Commons.

McGuinness had been a lieutenant in 'C' Company of the 1st Dublin Battalion. During Easter Week his company had surprised an escort of Lancers[2] who were guarding a convoy of ammunition and had driven them to an improvised shelter. When the British had pushed down Church Street, they had occupied a post which the Volunteers had evacuated and which gave them good fire control. He had shown fine courage in leading men to reseize a barricade from which they had been previously driven under heavy fire. McGuinness was known to the electors by a photograph in Volunteer uniform and by his convict cap and convict number on posters, and these had to supply the presence of the usual candidate whose presence was expected to add considerable weight to his chances, for he could promise a slice of the moon to anyone before the votes were counted.

The IPP candidate, Paddy McKenna, was well known and popular. He was a pig buyer well known to the other farmers. There was a fairly large Unionist population in the county, and they would be sure to have a vote. They too might help the IPP who made use of the Union Jack, perhaps to draw their vote, but if there was any fear of a convict rebel being returned, their votes would be a certainty.

Volunteers had come from all over Ireland to work for their candidate. North Roscommon, which had already been through a successful election, had a number of experienced canvassers and speakers, and as they were close by, a fair number of them were put up in friendly houses. Many of the strangers were released prisoners. At that time Easter Week had a significance of effort which was fresh in people's memories and anyone who 'had been out' that week had a strange status. People would come from a long distance either to look at him or talk to him. The daily and weekly papers were either imperialist or friendly to the IPP. But rumour and the winged word could amplify or distort a phrase according as it was for or against. The folklore recording of events was set in opposition to the printed page. Very few country people then read a daily paper, and that in itself helped the word of mouth by an absence of competition. Ballads made up for any gaps in information by playing on the emotions and as there had been numerous songs written about 1916, voices in full throat could obstruct a rival meeting as effectively as ashplants. Irish Volunteers worked as canvassers, organised and got ready transport or made the preliminary arrangements for meetings. These Volunteers from the outside and the Longford men had an extra incentive to work as hard as they could for they knew that the selection of a candidate was a challenge to the authority which kept McGuinness in prison for fighting in arms. If McGuinness failed to win his seat, it would seem like a repudiation of one of their men behind bars, and if any extra spur were needed to give an effort, this was the spur.

The Royal Irish Constabulary, with rolled up greatcoats and beehive helmets, were brought in by train from surrounding counties. They carried their carbines, ammunition and bayonets. A fine force they looked as they marched from the railway station to the neighbouring barracks or as they tramped through the streets to protect meetings. Their protection too often meant that they guarded the IPP meetings but did not interfere when McGuinness supporters were being attacked by the baton men, who carried a rather nice piece of lead in the core of their short bludgeons to help the strength of their arms. They had had their daily parades in their own barracks, and their regular musketry courses to keep their hands in tune with their rifles and revolvers. Their height was increased by their swarthy appearances and by the porter bottle colour of their uniforms. They were commanded by District Inspectors who had usually served as officers in the British army.

The quiet years before the First World War had made the Royal Irish Constabulary more opaque. The fathers of Volunteers had seen the RIC armed presence defending bailiffs with their battering rams as they levelled cottages, or as a protection to landlords, their agents and parasites. They had seen them charge with the bayonet or flail with their batons, as their grandfathers again had seen them use their carbines in the Tithe War.[3] In the years close to 1916 the RIC, except in land trouble or in the protection of recruiting meetings, had been quiet servants of the Crown. After 1916 they had picked up for arrest the men who had been for years in their secret report files and again they were arresting men for singing 'The Wearing of the Green', 'whistling derisively' at them, or for bearing names in Irish on crimson carts. They were still the symbol of British authority, which could be legal or ruthless when their masters advised or ordered. The sergeant was a man of authority to whom it was a pleasure for many a man to stand a pint or a drop of malt on a fair day. His large moustache even when dewy from his appreciation of a dark pint could yet quiver with a foreboding of what lay behind law. His weighty words and his extravagant use of ponderous English was respectfully listened to, for had he not authority or, more important, influence? Was not he on speaking terms with the great, with solicitors, doctors, ex-British officers and Justices of the Peace? An apocryphal story, perhaps, which went the rounds describes a sergeant moving on four men chatting at a corner 'Move on there now, move on I tell you and don't be collaborating in multitudes'.

The visiting Irish Volunteers helped to bolster the men in local companies who were eager to help, but whose parade discipline was uneven and unceremonious. Strange officers took them for route marches so as to converge them with other companies for election meetings. Their respect for the Royal Irish Constabulary or fear of their power was reduced for new recruits when they were drilled in front of them by strangers. Their own officers gained confidence and assurance in the handling of men and were impressed by the humorous jauntiness of the outside officers and of their thorough disrespect for the RIC. Seán Connolly could see this change and, like many a budding officer, he made good use of the election interval to learn all he could from men, who once but a rumour, had now become his friends. Friendship was quickly given and accepted then. It was easy to be direct and on easy terms of talk or of work with these men from the outside.

The attentive eyes of the bottle-green RIC stored away facial descriptions of the strangers, and they watched sardonically the lads whose houses they had visited to collect dog licences or to fill up tillage forms while their seemingly harmless questions compiled other information also. Contempt for this play-acting of the Volunteers was mixed with a now dubious observance of the impersonal manner in which the county and the townsmen now carried out orders, and the steady way in which they met attacks from Ancient Order of Hibernians and from the formidable invective, punctuated with empty porter bottles and stones.

The Irish Volunteers had come into action in Limerick when a parade of the Limerick City Regiment, strengthened by Volunteers from Cork, Dublin and from neighbouring counties, had marched through the city on the Whit Monday of 1915. The relatives of men, serving mainly in the Royal Munster Fusiliers, waited until the Volunteers had reached an historic spot, Mungret Street, where Limerick women were supposed to have hurled back the Williamites who had poured through the breached walls. With bottles and stones the Limerick women tried to break up the lines of marching men. Sir Henry Wilson was to spend that same July 12th at Currygrane House, at his brother's place near Ballinalee. Then he had come across to Galway to greet Lord (John) French there. They were both met by the separation women[4] from the Irish-speaking Claddagh, not with broken bottles, but with shouts of 'Long live the King. Long live England'. The Claddagh men, like others in a number of coastal towns in West Cork, had served for generations in the British navy.

It was dangerous to wear a tricolour ribbon in the streets of Longford as an attempt would be made to tear it from lapels or from hats. Republican women had to be protected from the separation women who had been particularly upset in this garrison town of Longford. Organisers from the Ancient Order of Hibernians had told them that if the Sinn Féiner was elected their separation money would be stopped. That was bad news for thirsty throats whose hopeful toast was 'Here's to the war that it may never end'.

Easter Week had shaken people out of their political apathy. It had made them question British intentions and promises. They had begun to question other organisations, such as the Ancient Order of Hibernians and the Irish Parliamentary Party. Political opponents could not understand the unrest occasioned by Easter Week, the doubt it engendered, or the speed with which support of and admiration for that forlorn hope had spread. During the election in early May a letter was published in the Irish papers which gave cause for great talk throughout South Longford. Sixteen Catholic bishops, three Protestant bishops, the Archbishop of Dublin and Cardinal Michael Logue had signed their names to a manifesto which asked that people should now publish their allegiance to an undivided country and not for the Irish Parliamentary Party which had agreed to the partition of the country.

> We appeal to the people without distinction, religious or political, and we ask all who are opposed to partition, temporary or permanent, to send their names. To Irishmen of every creed and class and party, the very thought of our country partitioned and torn as a new Poland, must be one of heart-rending sorrow.

The mixture of Catholic and Protestant names showed that unease at British proposals was uniting men who believed in an undivided

Ireland. To the youth after the Second World War, Partition means an occasional remembrance when a politician begins to make use of it, usually for party purposes, but in 1917 the dismemberment of an historic nation which had lived as a unit in men's minds, caused acute distress. It was remembered that even though central authority was weak under native rule, there was the mental concept of the country as a whole, which could be symbolised by the literary tradition of a chief poet who was free to wander through warring provinces.

A letter from Dr William Walsh, the Archbishop of Dublin, appeared in the papers on 8 May, the day before the election. He had mentioned that the Irish Parliamentary Party had agreed to Partition and that the country was practically sold. The Dublin *Evening Herald* brought the Archbishop's letter to Ballymahon that evening. Seán Milroy was a Sub-Director of Elections working under Dan MacCarthy. Paddy Morrissey was sent through the town to try to find Milroy to give him the important news. There was a long search for the Subdirector, but he was found at last where he could be expected to be found. Morrissey had cycled down from Dublin with four other Easter Week men, including Ernie Noonan of the London Irish, who having come over from England to fight, had been trained in Larkfield before the Rising and had then been attached to the 4th Battalion. Milroy decided that handbills would have to be printed that night but the nearest printing office which had friendly workmen was the Athlone Printing Works. Paddy Morrissey was sent off in a motor car with Brian Martin, an Athlone man who would help in finding people he knew there. Chapman, the Protestant manager of the works, was friendly, but then the printers had to be rounded up. They had gone home or were visiting, but Mulvihill, who lived out of the country, helped to track down compositors, and soon after eleven o'clock at night men were busy at the printing work, setting type by hand.

By three o'clock in the morning one thousand copies were printed. Morrissey hurried back to Ballymahon with his posters, throwing them at the crossroads, leaving a few here and there at friendly houses with the assurance that they would be posted up at once. Soon the walls leading to all small towns and villages were plastered with Dr Walsh's letter. Another 5,000 handbills came in from Athlone at eleven o'clock that morning. The Archbishop's name and his rank must have swayed many a voter that day either to attend the poll, or to 'vote for the man in jail'. The manager of the works, to add to his helpful assistance, refused to take money for the printing of the letter.

Outside the courthouse, inside of which votes were being counted, there was a packed crowd who were at peace in the excitement of waiting for the count to finish. It was the custom then that the election placard of the candidate who had won would be thrown out of the courthouse window as a sign of victory. Suddenly before the expectant eyes of the crowd McGuinness's placard came out the window. Small Union Jacks were waved as the Redmondites waved and shouted their delight but mired with their exuberance were bitter taunts about 'German gold' and 'baby killers', which put the Volunteers in the crowd in a fighting mood. Then big John O'Mahony came to the window. He held up his hand for silence, but the victorious Irish Parliamentary Party yell hid his voice, but it would have required more than a yell to hide his rotund and imperturbable figure. When he was able to make himself heard he shouted 'the flag of Ireland is not down yet'. Then Dan McCarthy spoke. He had asked for a recount, he said. The Redmondites were satisfied that their man had won, but when the new result came a little later showing that McGuinness had won by 37 votes, the Irish Parliamentary Party men and women melted like snow in a thaw. From then on the streets of Longford were controlled by the Republicans who had won against the heavy odds of a hostile press, local clergy, a well-paid organisation and ample support.

There were a few visits by Michael Collins to the county where he met Volunteers and discussed the gaps in the organisation of the Volunteers in the Longford Brigade. He addressed a meeting near Granard and as a result of this speech, which was an incentive to join the Volunteers and to use arms, the police in the county and in Dublin were on the look out for him, but he was not found for some time. Thomas Ashe made a speech in Ballinalee on the hill. A big crowd listened to him, but he did not make a fiery speech, if anything it was moderate. The size of the crowd may have prevented the RIC from taking notes. Sometimes, it was not advisable for a man in uniform or in plain clothes to be seen with a notebook in hand at a meeting, but there was a legal remedy by which notes which were not taken could be used. A Royal Irish Constabularyman was permitted in court to quote from his memory. He could listen to the speech and take 'mental notes'. It was on the 'mental notes' of a Constable Bowers from Cavan that Thomas Ashe was afterwards sentenced in September, 1917, to one year with hard labour.

The Volunteers recruited slowly. The first impetus was the South Longford election, the next one was soon to come. In April of 1918 a military service bill, the Conscription Act, was passed. All that was needed to make it applicable to Ireland was an Order-in-Council. The Irish Parliamentary Party voted against the bill, then finding that their presence in Westminister was of little use in opposition to conscription they left the House of Commons and returned to Ireland. The Prime Minister, David Lloyd George, sardonically introduced the Manpower Bill the same day the report of the Irish Convention, which had been meeting for the past eight months, was placed on the table of the Commons. It was evident that he had not read the report. The Convention which had been attended by all Irish parties except Sinn Féin, and many representatives of public bodies who would be defeated at an election, had recommended the immediate enforcement of a measure of self government. A subcommittee had reported that the conscription would be impossible without the consent of an Irish Parliament. Lloyd George in his strange way had said 'when the young men of Ireland had been brought in large numbers into the firing line, it is important that they should feel that they were not fighting for the purpose of establishing a principle abroad, which is denied to them at home'.

British divisions had been thinned by a murderous warfare in which both heavyweights on the French front slogged away dourly determined but without any brilliant solution to the stalemate of trench warfare. It was natural that England should squeeze Ireland to keep her promise in replacements to the French who had suffered most. The Easter Rising had dried up the channel of voluntary recruits, and it had acted as a signpost which had led away from the indifferent imperial bloody highway into a single track of its own interest. As is usual in the imperial conception of history, the use of a spate of Irish blood in the imperial interest is accepted, but the small trickle spilt in an effort for freedom at home is always enlarged upon as a crime against morality and humanity.

In Dublin delegates from Sinn Féin, the Trades Union Conference and the two sections of the Irish Parliamentary Party met in conference, and they decided to oppose this threat. A pledge to resist conscription was taken after Mass on Sunday[5] at all chapels and two days later a general strike took place throughout Ireland, with the exception of a small part of Ulster. That was an effective protest. All transport was involved from jaunting car to railway trains.

The Irish Volunteers had now to act as a shelter belt for recruits who suddenly made up their minds to join up. Some companies doubled, trebled and played with the multiplication table until the number of men on parade was sometimes fifteen times the normal number. Many of the recruits would have been a hindrance in action as local officers were not competent to train and discipline large numbers of raw men whose spirit was primarily concerned with their own welfare. The Royal Irish Constabulary were not secure in their own minds. They saw that the people were determined to resist by any means they considered feasible and that desperation could give determination. There was a shortage of arms. Since the Rising an odd soldier home on leave had either left his rifle behind him or he had been disarmed. After a series of such losses soldiers were not allowed to bring home their rifles when on leave in Ireland. Even the National Volunteers had been disarmed. In some areas they had good service rifles, but the Irish Parliamentary Party was as anxious to get rid of rifles as the British were to impound them. All weapons were overhauled, and quartermasters who had neglected to inspect weapons were now confronted with the disastrous effect of this damp climate on shotguns and small arms. Some shopkeepers handed over cartridges, caps and shotguns, detonators and fuses. Gunpowder was manufactured in many varying mixtures of efficiency and disaster. Shotgun cartridges were emptied and refilled with buckshot. Grenades were made from tin cans filled with broken pieces of pot packed around a cylindrical depression, which in time would receive a stick of gelignite with a detonator and fuse. The tins could be strengthened by flanges and bolts. They made a nice little explosion when thrown and might be useful in a street crowded with enemy but the proud owner of such a grenade was as content as if he had control of a trench mortar. Blacksmiths hammered out pikes as their ancestors had worked at them one hundred twenty years previously in 1798, and again in 1867. Pike handles were abstracted from plantations with or without permission.

Surveys were made of foodstuffs in shops and storehouses and of transport and petrol supplies. Staff work was built up out of this accumulation of details which had to be systematised to be of use. In Longford there had been instructions sent on by Rory O'Connor, Director of Engineering, as to how railways, rolling stock, culverts and bridges were to be destroyed with and without explosives. Long memos were read on the subject of demolition, but the only sources of supply for explosives were the county council quarries which usually kept gelignite or blasting gelatin, and the home made powder. Soon the quarries had to place their explosive material in the nearest RIC barracks for there had been an epidemic of raids on the small supply. The Cumann na mBan made splints, dressings and bandages. They made haversacks, bandoliers and first aid outfits, and they helped to bake barley bread which was an emergency ration. Barley bread had been used by the old people. It was very good, they said, in their reminiscent way. Some of the barley which I tried on companies who remained out for a day's training would also turn the contents of a refilled buckshot cartridge.

Dispatches were sent on foot, on bicycles, or by horses to test lines of communication from company to company. Every company had a call house and at functions three or four dispatch riders had to be always on duty. Soon the lines tightened up and as every dispatch was accompanied by its time sheet it was easy to check on lapsed time, but big time sheets suffered on their way from Dublin to Longford as they parted for Mayo, Sligo and Donegal.

At his Dublin office in Bachelors' Walk, Michael Collins had large maps of Ireland on which the through routes stretching out from Dublin were marked on in different colours. There were weak spots on most lines because companies were careless, or their officers were indifferent. His curses concentrated as he jabbed at a particular map patch which gave trouble, or he called down fervently the name of some officer whom he could blame for delays, as he strode up and down the room. His office, which was a general clearing place as well for communications organisation and quartermasters temporary stores, had been raided suddenly one morning. Collins was arrested in Dublin for the speech he had once made at Legga in early March. He was brought under police arrest to Granard, where he was tried by a civil court, and as he refused to give bail he was sentenced to some months in prison. While he was in Sligo Jail it was decided by the Volunteer Executive, as conscription was then a menace, that Volunteer officers and men who were in prison as a result of their refusal to give bail could now allow bail to be handed over for their release. Collins and others were released when their money guarantee of good behaviour was paid over to the court, but some prisoners refused to give this bail.

To a detached observer these parades of men, faultily drilled, armed with brush handles or hurleys, decorated with undyed haversacks which would locate their proud owners quickly at long range, seemed to be a bluff. He would think in terms of their opponents, the well-drilled Royal Irish Constabulary and the butt-clattering British soldiers who now held not only garrison towns but workhouses and railway stations. The seriousness of the marching men was often a check to mocking doubt, and the tenseness of the people meant that war was judged by the standard of their determination to resist. Irish soldiers who came home on leave were disturbed. Their own families were involved and on their return to their regiments a certain unrest had set in.

There was the story of the English correspondent who had come to Dublin to get an idea of Irish resistance to the Manpower Bill. He was drinking his late morning coffee in the Dublin Bread Company restaurant when his eye caught the reversed letters D.B.C. on the window. Curious as to what the letters meant he called over his waitress and he asked her what they stood for. '"Death Before Conscription", that's what they stand for', she replied, and the startled face of the visitor gave assent to another Dublin tale.

There had been a swoop by the British in May 1918, but it was not as sudden a swoop as they had intended it to be. Information that there was something pending at the Dublin Castle had been sent both to Harry Boland and Michael Collins by two of the 'G' Division men there who had begun to give information of what they saw, heard or noticed in documents. On Friday 17 May, the information had become more definite. Military lorries were waiting in the Lower Castle Yard and detectives had been instructed to accompany them on raids to houses which they knew in Dublin. There was a meeting of the Volunteer Executive that evening and the information was passed on to the members, some of whom had come up from the country. Eamon de Valera, who had been appointed President of the Irish Volunteers at the last Convention, was also told. It was decided to avoid arrest of those present, but de Valera was also at the time President of Sinn Féin. Collins and Cathal Brugha, both on the Volunteer Executive, were also members of the Executive Committee of Sinn Féin.

There had also been a meeting of the Sinn Féin Executive that morning. They had been warned by Harry Boland that their names were on the raiding list. After a long discussion the Sinn Féin Executive decided that they would go home where they would wait to be arrested. If they went 'on their keeping', as avoidance of arrest was then and formerly called, they felt they would not be able to attend to their many committee meetings and to work which required publicity, but they each appointed substitutes who would replace them. Papers were removed from No. 6 Harcourt Street and men said goodnight to each other as they went home wondering in what jail they would next meet. At home they had time to burn or carefully hide papers and to pack their bags for a journey before the heavy footed men of the 'G' Division came to identify and arrest them, backed by military who waited on the outside. In the ordinary progression of restrictions people had to learn to both avoid arrest and manage to carry out their office work at the same time. The Sinn Féin organisation itself was suppressed within two months' time and the substitutes in its ranks who replaced the arrested men had to keep out of jail.

The arrests were later explained as part of complicity in a 'German Plot'. That plot was specially to withdraw any sympathy or interest, which Americans might have had in such a large number of representative men being arrested and deported. There had been a man captured who had landed from a collapsible boat on the coast of Clare on 12 April. He had a message for the Irish leaders, but Joseph Dowling, the arrested man, could have given it to the British, for whom it was really meant, but he did not. That was the flimsy excuse on which the arrests were based. Previously, the Chief Secretary had been changed, the Viceroy was replaced by Lord French, the Commander-in-Chief had been removed. All these changes evidently meant that conscription was to be enforced and the removal of the Irish leaders was the first step in that game. In addition, the removal of leaders might make it easier for the British to break up resistance to conscription. Joe McGuinness who had been acting as Director of Elections in East Cavan when Arthur Griffith was a candidate, was now a candidate, and had also been arrested with a number of his assistants. There had been police raids all over the country, it was found out within the next few days. The prisoners were sent to seven jails in England, perhaps to break up their numbers and to minimise possibly concerted action.

Michael Collins and Cathal Brugha avoided capture. Out of these arrests began the real influence of Collins, who was on the Supreme Council of the Irish Republican Brotherhood. Now that a number of people, who were opposed to the IRB, had been removed by the British, there was less check on the infiltration of its members into positions which would give them additional power. By the end of 1918 they had been able to influence the selection of many of the Parliamentary candidates in the general election, yet the decision of Sinn Féin Clubs to nominate prisoners as candidates probably overruled some of the IRB selections. De Valera, who did not know he had been selected, had been their candidate as President of Sinn Féin in opposition to Arthur Griffith in 1917. They had gone around each major Sinn Féin voting group before the Convention to arrange for candidates for resolutions. Brugha who had been in the IRB no longer believed in its use. He was Chief-of-Staff of the IRA and the genesis of his clash with Collins would appear to come from Collins's many IRB activities, which often made use of the Staff Department without cut and dried permission from the Chief-of-Staff.

The RIC had been at first uneasy about the Manpower Bill, but as raids for arms increased and raids for Volunteer officers who had handled men in public, they fell into their usual authoritarian groove. They had been present at all public meetings and parades, and they had forwarded their accumulative information on every aspect of Irish life which was considered hostile to the British. Longford was made a proclaimed district, and in July a month later Sinn Féin, the Cumann na mBan, the Gaelic League, and the Irish Volunteers were proclaimed. All of these organisations, two of which were definitely pacific were included in the reason for their suppression: 'that they did encourage and aid persons to commit crime and incite to acts of violence and intimidation, and interfere with the administration of the law and disturb the maintenance of law and order'. Soon afterwards meetings, assemblies and processions could not be held save police officers gave permission in writing. Even Gaelic football and hurling matches came under this ban, as no organisation would ask a County Inspector for his permission to hold a meeting, or to play a football match. On the one day the Gaelic Athletic Association held matches all over Ireland without a permit, the British were not able to suppress such a number of events, and they did not interfere. This suppression of meetings led to baton and bayonet charges and to resultant raids and arrests. There was a tendency on the part of the RIC and of the military to open fire when they tried to disperse meetings which refused to recognise their authority.

In spite of proclamations meetings were attended. Placards would be posted up in a town stating that a monster Sinn Féin meeting or rally would be held in a certain town on a certain date. The British would proclaim the meeting and their posters which had been plastered around the town would be in disconnected strips the next morning. Early on the day in question military and Royal Irish Constabulary would move into the town. Roads leading outwards would be held by pickets behind sandbagged defences while bayoneted sentries exposed themselves. The centre of the town would be used by military minds to think in, assisted by machine guns and parked transport.

A few miles away people who had already been advised through Sinn Féin Clubs or Volunteers would converge on a field which had been the selected centre. There, protected by scouts on horseback and on bicycles, the real meeting took place, while in the defended town only the wind was allowed to make noise. As there were no RIC now to take mental notes, a speaker could threaten the British Empire and its local potentates to the delight of his expectant audience.

The British reply to this evasion was to proclaim an area. This would give them power to break up any meetings which they might come across within a wide radius. It also meant they would have to use a good number of troops and constabulary. Small groups which constituted a skeleton meeting would lead the Crown forces across country, when the civilians would be found to be interested in the dexterity of pitch and toss or preoccupied with a very serious game of '21'. In the distance or on a hilltop another group with tricolour flags would be trailed by exasperated soldiers, who would find further on men in shirt sleeves throwing a half hundred to the shouts of encouragement by an audience of girls. The decoy groups had done their work, while at a crossroads or in a conveniently sheltered field the well attended meeting was held. All these circumambient movements gave the people who attended a secret to hold. They were as a result trained to avoid talk to prevent leakage of information, while they passed on all aspects of British movement, protected by Volunteer outposts which observed, reported and moved carefully.

The British pressure to force Irishmen to fight for them was determined by their heavy losses and by their inability to replace casualties. Politically, they had to watch the effect their actions might have or they could embarrass the United States which had not yet sent men to fight. To placate criticism a Convention was kept talking and now that American forces could be hoped for in Europe some kind of a Home Rule Bill had to be discussed to keep quiet anti-Woodrow Wilson American pressure. In March 1918, Winston Churchill and Alfred Milner were strongly in favour of Irish conscription, but Jan Christiaan Smuts, Bonar Law, George Barnes and Lloyd George were waiting for the report of the Irish Convention. President Woodrow Wilson who was expected to send 120,000 American infantry to France for three months had shown the British Cabinet that his difficulties would have been increased by Irish conscription. Sir Henry Wilson, however, then Chief of the Imperial General Staff, was not afraid of the thought of mixing 150,000 recalcitrant Irishmen among the two and a half million soldiers of the British Empire.

On 6 April the United States had declared war on Germany, but not until 25 June did the first American landing take place. In May, Lloyd George wished that Ireland was at the bottom of the sea. He advised the new Viceroy Lord French to put the onus for the first shooting on the rebels. He decided he would place the Manpower Bill on the table of the House of Commons on the same day as he placed the Orders-in-Council there. Lord French was very helpful to Cabinet doubters for he was quite confident he would be ready for anything that occurred in Ireland. In July, Lord French decided that he would conscript the Irish in October, and he was anxious to have Ulster Volunteer rifles handed over to secret Ulster armories. By the end of September, the British had been victorious in the Near East and the Bulgarians had given up the fight, yet on 1 October, Sir Henry Wilson met Lord French and others in London where they made plans to enforce conscription.

In the dark hours of the morning of 15 October, British troops took over houses in Dublin and held canal and river bridges leading out from the city. Tanks rumbled up and down, armoured cars threatened with their armour, and pickets were alert as if ready for action. From midnight telegraphic staffs in towns and cities were on duty waiting for orders, which would, when they reached the nearest posts or barracks, instruct Crown forces how to begin. All day the troops waited but no Orders-in-Council were laid on the table of the House of Commons. The Germans were preparing to surrender but conscription for Ireland was advocated by Sir Henry Wilson as a means for supplying needed manpower as a threat to German disarmament, and also for a removal of young men who could continue to cause trouble in Ireland. Towards the end of the month all the understanding that Sir Henry Wilson could obtain from Churchill and Lloyd George was that conscription would be applied at once if the Germans did not surrender their arms.

Lord French and Sir Henry Wilson saw no difficulties in the enforcing of conscription. Both knew the military machine thoroughly but neither was responsible for the political consequences of a determined and ruthless action. The result of Easter Week had a lesson in it for regulars who believed in resolute government, but professional soldiers judge by results mostly in relation to their effects on other professional soldiers. The English Cabinet on the other hand had had to weigh up each Sinn Féin and each Redmondite victory at the polls, to make members of a Convention juggle with words where some of the representatives on it represented nothing more than themselves. Losses at the front and the effect of President Wilson's Irish American Democratic backing of drastic measures in Ireland had constantly to be thought of. The President had been inscrutable even to the British ambassador in Washington. He had once in a speech described the European war as 'a drunken brawl in a public house', and the ambassador had reported that as a result of his practically never seeing ambassadors of 'the mysterious way in which he makes anything a matter of divination rather than diplomacy'.

Easter Week 1916, the forlorn hope, had by then doubly justified itself as far as the saving of Irish lives was concerned. Since 1914 recruiting had slowed to a small trickle, and in 1918, when conscription would have been enforced only for the threat of resistance, that threat was again based on the Rising in Dublin. After the Armistice of 11 November 1918 the big numbers at Volunteer parades fell away quickly. All a man had to do was not to attend his mobilisation order for a series of parades. If he wished to leave the Volunteers, he could leave not by the method of refusing to carry out orders, but by quietly ignoring them. By the end of November the numbers of men carrying out their routine orders fell in mathematical inexactitude. The number of men in the Longford Brigade had increased as compared with the days before the threat when men had served because they desired to serve, but any recruits who remained on soon caught that strange Volunteer spirit which made them men apart.

Chapter 3

Longford and National Developments, 1918–20

————

In 1919, Pat Garrett, an instructor, was sent down by GHQ to teach drill and the use of arms in Longford. He had served for a long while in the British army and as with old soldiers his knowledge had become instinctive. There were a few rifles in the Longford Brigade. These now were passed around from company to company for the men to make use of. Very few men had had a rifle previously in their hands, for rifle knowledge, with a few exceptions, belonged to men who had served with the British in the last war. It seems strange that there could be a few rifles in a battalion and that men would not know its mechanism or have been taught the triangle of error test to help them in taking a proper sight. I had been in a company in the 1st Dublin Battalion, but I had not seen recruits instructed even in the mechanism of a rifle, though I had heard our captain evolve the principle of the use of sights.

Observation of objects and their indication, use of military vocabulary to increase accuracy of description, judging distances and the making of range-cards could have given an added interest to the men. That training would have brought them out in their own countryside to study over ground which they might later have had to fight over. Rifles had to be hidden away for safety, but that reason for keeping arms out of men's hands would have increased threefold due to the persistence of raids up to the end of 1920. After that date rifles were on the backs of men, yet there were many

Volunteers who in 1921 had never had the mechanism of a grenade or of an automatic explained to them.

Garrett went from company to company. He avoided the towns so as not to excite suspicion and to avoid the natural curiosity at a stranger's presence. He could interest the men, by his trained experience, and he saw that weapons were kept clean. He taught bayonet fighting with brush handles or straight lengths of branches while he lilted the time to the men. He kept moving about when the brigade was reorganised, and when the column was busy, and he was still instructing in the area when the Truce came along in July 1921.

Seán Connolly was Vice Commandant of the North Longford 1st Battalion, which covered a wide area of ground.[1] His Commandant was Seán MacEoin who had been at school with him. Connolly was now 29. That seemed young enough but judged by the average Volunteer age at the time, he was almost elderly. He became interested in codes and ciphers. Messages then were sent in code to military and police. If there were sympathetic people in a post office a copy of the messages which passed through could be handed over frequently. In Longford Post Office there were friendly girls who sent out copies of telegrams and of telephone messages. They were alert for anything which might concern the local British garrison. Often enough the code word was supplied by a District Inspector's clerk, or it was sent on from our GHQ. It was difficult to obtain, as it was carefully guarded, but in 1919 and early 1920, the code word was not changed frequently.

Connolly was interested in codes. He thought that practice in coding and decoding would become more useful in time, and he was anxious to train himself by practices. When Frank Davis went to Dublin in the autumn on a double errand, Connolly was able to tell him when he returned that messages concerning him had been sent on to the RIC, and that enquiries had been made about him by the 'G' Division in Dublin. Davis was then being looked for by the

RIC in Longford. He had gone to the city to attend a motor engineering school and in addition he had been picked to take part in an attack on the Viceroy, Lord French.

A number of men from outside brigades had been selected for this work by the Supreme Council of the IRB. Possibly it was thought that a representative group was needed, but the Dublin Brigade was not over anxious for outside men to be present in the city, waiting. Thomas MacCurtain, who was then in charge of Cork No. 1 Brigade, had also been on the same errand. The Cork city RIC knew that he had been absent from Cork on one occasion when men were in position to ambush Lord French. He was not in Dublin on the occasion of the attack on the Viceroy although the military stated he was in the metropolis, but the RIC were able to prove he had been at home.

Davis had joined the IRB early in 1919, and when he had been sworn in at Seán MacEoin's house a Dublin visitor was present as was Seán Connolly. MacEoin was the local centre.[2] The Organisation had helped to prepare for Easter Week in Dublin, but it had also helped to unmake Easter Week in the provinces. 'The Organisation', as it was called, was of use to build up groups in other organisations and to try to get its men into key positions. It was particularly strong in the Gaelic Athletic Association. The IRB issued its own instructions, and it kept in touch with men in areas which were not active, or whose senior officers did not belong to the secret society. As fighting began, men had to develop by themselves, and 'the Organisation' became less of an influence, for an IRB man did not necessarily mean a good soldier. Yet it kept men isolated, who could, in touch with each other, be used for foreign communications or for the smuggling in of explosives, arms and ammunition, in Great Britain and in America. It could pick men for service in England, and its main influence was that men on the resident Volunteer Executive who lived in and around Dublin, and members of the GHQ Staff belonged to it.

Irish people mature slowly. That may be due to the influence of climate and the nature of the countryside. Our trees, shrubs and food supplies partake of this slow growth and as well there is the isolation of impact due to being on the European fringe, to the political lack of power, to the need of intellectual ferment conditioned by ancient seats of learning and the want of creative impulses.

The idea of steady continuous resistance in active warfare was foreign to the Irish nature due to their lack of development of a centralised authority which could control the forces of the provinces. There was a mental concept of the national struggle drawn from resistance to accumulative British aggression and from successive defeats for many centuries. Hugh O'Neill's Nine Years War[3] had been the first determined organised fight between the Irish and Anglo-Irish. Since that time, with the exception of the Williamite Wars, there had been the idea of a Rising, when whatever strength there was would rise out, learning of warfare in the then and there. That had been the history of waiting for foreign landings, of 1798, 1848, 1867, and then 1916. A country of slow growth was to pitch itself into war against trained soldiers. Our own history had proved the drawbacks to that form of the sudden burst out, by divided council, leakage of information and the lack of decision when untrained leaders of untrained men have to decide quickly and decisively. Another fact that made or seemed to make men more fearful of the heart of fight was the consequent increase in technical training implied by the complicated mechanism of weapons and of their growth in range. The trained soldier was becoming more and more a specialist.

The 1916 fighting had been the fulfilment of the ideal from the traditional viewpoint. On a fixed day there had been a rising out,[4] but with a small number of men, under fairly well-trained officers, when courage and enthusiasm had bridged the lack of efficiency. In that fight outposts from Clanwilliam House to the Mendicity and

King Street in Dublin had inflicted most of the casualties while the large battalion headquarters had kept the bulk of the men. That in itself the use of small bodies thrown out of a larger centre for protection duty was the chief lesson that might be learned. These small groups had the advantage of surprise and in many instances they took the offensive. The surrender of arms after the Rising was over was the biggest blow to any further attempt at armed resistance. Dublin, Cork, Limerick and a few other places surrendered over 1,400 rifles.

In 1917 and through 1918 the hope of a simultaneous outbreak lingered on in men's minds. At a Volunteer Convention in the autumn the assembled delegates authorised their Executive to declare war when it was considered necessary. Evidently the underlying menace of conscription had made this alteration. In 1918 conscription gave an added incentive to the gathering of all kinds and shapes of what might be called weapons, but what shape the general fight would take would depend on what information the Irish Volunteers could extract of British intentions. There would be additional information, it was felt, about British proposed activity, as the Dublin Metropolitan Police and many of the Royal Irish Constabulary would have been able to send out local information which would have helped as a preliminary to circumvent military and police operations. In Dublin it was thought the military would make simultaneous raids for leaders and for men. The city had been divided into blocks which would have to fight sector by sector.

By the end of 1918 the conception of what form a fight would take had changed. Since 1917 the British had taken the offensive. They had isolated districts such as Limerick and Westport by martial law. They had to back their authority with bayonets to enforce any of their regulations while republicans ignored their numerous printed prohibitions and proclamations. For each month of 1918 the average arrest was 94 and the average number of men and women sentenced to periods of imprisonment was 70. The enforcing of British decrees meant a continuous use of troops, arrests and raids; the protection of courts and court-martials meant an additional parade strength of British soldiers and RIC.

A considerable energy was used up in making certain aspects of English rule difficult, but the real unity of purpose was hammered out on the anvil of the prison cell. For three years, 1917, 1918, and 1919, prisoners were the front line. Men who had been a name met comrades from Kerry to Belfast, and through continuous discussion a unity of outlook was formed and a rigorous jail discipline accepted. Afterwards the bond of friendship would continue when men were free, although they were as widely separated as were their counties. Men had met men whom they could trust, respect and admire, and when a Volunteer was fighting in isolation later on he knew his one time jail friends were in the same predicament, if over a hundred miles away.

In jail, improvisation and ingenuity – two normal Irish characteristics – were used in resisting attempts to treat prisoners as criminals. Members of the political Sinn Féin met Irish Volunteers and learned to take orders from Volunteer officers, and to obey even when the dreadful form of the hunger strike had to be used. Jail escapes heightened morale and gave the people a feeling that the British, whose system was thought to be irresistible, were being outwitted by men who were irrepressible. Also it gave expression to the ridiculous, which cannot be circled by bayonets.

The elections on 14 December 1918 gave six seats[5] to the Irish Parliamentary Party and 73 to Sinn Féin Republicans, yet IPP members had polled one vote to about every three and a half votes to Republicans, and Unionists had polled more votes than had the IPP. That aspect of the election was forgotten, I expect, when the total number of seats won by the different parties was examined, for Republicans held 70 per cent of the seats. The big bulk of the Nationalists during the ensuing two years were changed somewhat, but a good number had their own reservations about the wisdom of the policy of armed resistance. The British, however, endeavoured to wage war on the people themselves, taking every one they did not personally know to be hostile.

From January 1919 onwards when the General Headquarters Staff met under Cathal Brugha, as Chief-of-Staff, before he became Minister for Defence, decisions were often distributed to the IRA through articles in *An t-Oglach* which had been first published in August of 1918. Then it had stated: 'Volunteers are not politicians – they follow no political leaders as such, their allegiance is to the Irish Nation'. In January 1919, it further stated

> Dáil Éireann in its message to the Free Nations of the world declares a state of war to exist between Ireland and England. It further declares that that state of war can never be ended until the English invader vacates our country.
>
> Every Volunteer is entitled morally and legally when in the execution of his military duties to use all legitimate methods of warfare, in particular any policeman, soldier, judge, warder or official must be made to understand that it is not wise for him to distinguish himself by undue zeal in the service of England in Ireland.

An t-Oglach placed a heavy burden on the communication system. It was printed surreptitiously, though printing offices were continuously searched in an attempt to track it down. Then it was sent to every company in Ireland no matter how remote, but distribution within the brigade was the brigadier's work. Each issue was expected to be read to the men on parade.

Up to the end of 1919 the British had been the aggressors despite the few attacks on patrols and on posts. Meetings had been broken up with bayonets and the arm strength of Dublin Metropolitan Police and RIC batons. Raids had increased in number and the procedure adopted during the invasion had changed from harsh arrogance to a deliberate destruction. Now a house would have its floors broken up with crowbars and axes, and its interior might look as if a cyclone had struck it. Worse still, from the viewpoint of women and children, these raids took place mostly at night. Frightened children had electric light swung on to their faces and half dressed men and women were questioned. Resolute women followed the raiders from room to room. Pilfering of the housewife's egg money, and the sucking of stray eggs by soldiers, slowly entered the stage of looting when watches and jewelry, melodeons and clothing disappeared. The regulars led the way and their officers were indifferent save in journalistic centres such as Dublin, where robbery could have an appropriate comment. There had been an increasing number of men killed by rifle fire or by bayonets in every county. The slow accumulation of acts of aggression offset the slow approach towards a political background. Sinn Féin had had among its departments those of Food Control, Agriculture, Labour and Public Health, but in 1919 departments under An Dáil were staffed and began slowly to work. Their organisation was a necessary background to the development of a fight which in essence was to make the British distribute strength in defence of their institutions and an attempt to nullify their form of government by making it inoperative, first by attacking constabulary and then military who defended their system.

By this time people had learned that gossip and random talk about their own institutions led to the arrest of their sons and relatives. Men were now able to avoid arrest and to move through city and county without knowledge of their whereabouts being circulated. When arrested, prisoners denied the authority of the court or of the court martial to try them, and people began to avoid bringing their legal problems to be settled by the British courts. The civil and military wings of organisations which backed the Dáil were protected by a large number of people, and as time went on the people themselves had to bear the burden of this protection by providing food, contributing to levies for the buying of arms and the purchase of equipment for active men and columns.

In Dublin the General Headquarters Staff could suggest, yet someone had to begin and to take responsibility for operations. Once an area became active there would be an attempt to overawe it. Military and constabulary would display and use their arms, but if a brigade had a core of resistance then that core would strengthen with activity. Local planning depended upon local enterprise as was natural but the Volunteers were not soldiers, neither had they a uniform system of training or uniform weapons. Training was something that each interested man had to learn for himself save there were energetic officers. In some cities there was an approach to training through classes for officers, non-commissioned officers and for the Special Services. There was a Training Department at GHQ, which used columns in *An t-Oglach*, but not until 1921 were there definite classes in Dublin to train men who would be sent out to the country. Previously such training depended upon organisers who wandered about. The real training was the initiative to begin the trenching of a road, the holding up of mails for information or by attacks on positions or on forces in movement.

There had been a number of attacks on RIC barracks before the year 1920. In April of 1918 Kerrymen had rushed a hut in Gortlea, but although they had reached the rifles in the dayroom, a patrol out on duty had surprised them. They retreated with two dead men. That same month Eyeries Barracks in Co. Cork was captured with its arms. In 1919 Mid-Clare Brigade had attacked a number of huts but although they had wounded a number of RIC, they had not captured any arms, yet towards the end of the year Cooraclare

Barracks in Co. Clare had been destroyed by the use of mines. The guardroom in Collinstown Aerodrome had been surprised by the 1st Battalion of the Dublin Brigade who had captured 72 rifles, the largest seizure during the active fight. Bolivar RIC Barracks in Co. Meath had been captured in November by the Meath men.

In January 1920 the fashion of attacking barracks spread as suddenly and as unaccountably as fashions in women's clothing. Carrigatoher Barracks in Co. Tipperary was blown in with explosives while Araglin Barracks in Co. Cork was rushed suddenly and there were attacks on posts in seven counties.

.

Chapter 4

Longford, 1920
Drumlish, Mostrim, Ballinamuck, Top

———————

The first barracks attacked in Longford was on 6 January 1920 at Drumlish, close to the border of Co. Leitrim. The barracks was isolated and the intention was to use explosives on one gable end to demolish it. The post commanded the ground all around it for miles. Seán Connolly had sent his sister, Maura, to Dublin for arms and supplies, but like Mother Hubbard 'when she got there the cupboard was bare'. Cork had been given the arms which Connolly had expected to receive, but she got some Mills grenades, a revolver for her brother from Michael Collins, and a few odds and ends of war material. Seán met her at Edgeworthstown station but instead of the beaming welcome which she had expected as a result of bringing down the supplies in safety, her brother looked at her small hand cases and said sombrely 'Is that all you brought with you?'

There were explosives for the gable end and mines in reserve. These mines had been made from boxes of carts which had been collected through the battalion. Seán MacEoin had worked at his forge preparing flanges and bolts and these flanges had been placed at either end, strong bolts joined the ends together so as to strengthen the resistance of the metal to an explosive. Such a weapon could be made use of in a number of ways. It could be buried in the road to serve as a mine. When fully loaded it would weigh about nine or ten pounds. It could serve as a large grenade by packing broken scrap metal around the explosive, or it could be employed to blow in the door of a barracks while a storming party waited near by to rush in. Roads had been blocked by felling trees although the main road was not interfered with. The explosive for the end wall was carried up by Volunteers and was placed in position at the base of the gable. The fuse was ignited and the men quickly and quietly got back far enough to lie down so as to avoid whatever splinters of stone might come their way. The men who were to cover the barrack windows with shotguns and rifles waited for the explosion and the men who were to charge the breach were ready for their dash across, but nothing happened.

It was always dangerous to investigate a charge when for some reason, whether in fuse, detonator or explosives, there was a failure. The fault might be some kind of delay in result and an explosion might take place a considerable time later. Connolly took a cart box grenade and walked over towards the Drumlish Barracks door. There was a fanlight over the door and he could lob his cart box through the glass. At the time of this attack barracks generally around Ireland were not properly protected by steel plates. He tried to ignite the fuse but it would not light. After the third attempt he did hear the splutter that assured him, and the fizzle of light that told the waiting men that the fuse was lighting. He threw the bomb through the fanlight and the heavy box fell inside, but the clatter of the falling metal was the only satisfaction in sound anyone heard, for the explosive did not work.

The failure of the cart box may have been due to its metal case. In cold weather the metal would seep up the cold and retain it for a long time. The broken scrap inside could again spread the lower temperature which would freeze the gelignite in the centre of it, and frozen gelignite could not be detonated. In addition these improvised grenades had to be hidden in unsuspected places and the gelignite which should have been kept apart from the casing was only too often allowed to run the risk of a continuous contact. Rifle and shot gun fire was kept up for a while. The Royal Irish Constabulary, as was their custom, sent up a series of Very lights.[1] These whizzed up high above the barracks, made the neighbourhood incandescent and sent the warning of attack to neighbouring posts. But the British were careful about leaving their comfortable barracks at night. In Longford eight miles away there was a strongly held police barracks, the county headquarters of the RIC and two military barracks, but the county itself and the darkness were linked up to join the IRA outposts as an additional protection against an enemy advance. The garrison of this now isolated post was left to their own courage and fears until the light of day came slowly. After what was known in the newspapers as an interchange of shots, MacEoin, Connolly and the men with them made for their own districts.

There had been few arms except shotguns that night of the attack on Drumlish. The shot gun would have been the best weapon to stop any British advance to relieve a post in the night time, but it was not treated with the confidence it deserved. Private houses were now raided for arms by the IRA. The RIC had gathered up a fair share of weapons, but there were a number left perhaps for the safety of their owners. A miscellaneous collection of swords, spears, antique revolvers and good shotguns were gathered from the raids, but as constabulary and military raids on houses for Volunteers and for arms increased in number, the weapons had to depend on inadequate shelter from the dampness. Somehow sufficient ingenuity was not made use of to conceal weapons indoors. Mental alertness did not face this problem with any real agility, but on the other hand, the sons of a house would not usually be allowed to regard their home as a place for making weapons thoroughly secure and dry.

By this time in most counties the RIC had now withdrawn into the larger towns as it was felt they could not hold the more isolated posts against sporadic attacks. The military had proved that they were unable to reinforce a post between darkness and dawn. The IRA decided to take advantage of this situation.

The first general operation, which was carried out all over Ireland on the one day, 3 April, was the raiding of income tax offices for records and papers, and the destruction of vacated RIC barracks. The evening selected for the destruction and burning was Easter Saturday. That night the British, thoroughly prepared for another rising, were holding the outskirts of all cities and larger towns in Ireland. Something was due to happen they expected. Trains, motors, cars and carts were held up and searched as they came close to some cities, while passers by were also held up by pickets and patrols. Armoured cars and heavy lorries rattled up and down city streets. Armed patrols kept vigilant guard all through the nights of that Easter Week and while IRA destroyed papers, attempted to burn income tax offices and in the countryside where there were no longer police or military, the barracks blazed strongly. The daily papers of the following week read as if there had been simultaneous attacks on occupied barracks throughout Ireland. The Longford men had quietly collected petrol and paraffin. They had visited the neighbourhood of deserted barracks so that in each post there would be men who knew each room and the quickest method of burning the building. Cans of petrol and paraffin had to be gathered and concealed so that there would be no delay in the brigade timing for the start of conflagrations. Smear, in the hills towards the Cavan border, Field near Lough Gowna, and Ballinalee were destroyed in the North East of the county, and next day there were about seven posts remaining in the county instead of seventeen. There had been no serious accidents as had happened in other counties. There, men, who were unfamiliar with petrol, had splashed it on the walls and floors, and had then attempted to ignite the fluid. A number were burned to death and in a few cases men were blown out through the windows uninjured.

There were raids at once by the RIC and military. Seán Connolly, MacEoin and many other officers were searched for but although they had not been looked for up to this date, they were not now sleeping at home. Officers and men were now on the alert and raiding parties had to come from posts which were more remote. Usually raids took place in or about dawn and were guided by the labyrinthine country knowledge of the Royal Irish Constabulary; the hour before cock crow, when the ghosts left a house, was now the time when a man had to be most cautious about his very earthy successors.

The result of the bonfires and raids for papers was a feeling of security around Ireland. Over 300 barracks had been destroyed, a number of income tax offices in each county had been raided as were the houses of collectors, yet no Volunteer had been captured on any of the many operations of Easter Saturday night. The people understood that careful planning must have gone into the preparations for raids and for the destruction of posts yet there had been no leakage of information. The intelligence system, of the bottle green RIC gatherers of talk and gossip from the people, and then reports from paid agents and eager loyalists, had failed. This miscarriage of the RIC must have had an ominous effect in the Dublin Castle. The antennae which poked and pried into every secret nook in people's thoughts and the globose eye which turned on movement and even intention was beginning to disappoint its masters. In some areas where Volunteer officers were weak or inactive, the police had yet much of their old power. They could impress people, court the local girls and receive respect, yet even these police in their secure districts had not been able to ferret out the new type of Rising Out. The British had stolidly held towns and cities against the Irishry while in nearly all places held in force by them, income tax papers had been thoroughly destroyed. Some areas had not burnt their barracks nor had they taken the income tax papers. There had to be two subsequent operations in May so that Volunteer officers who had not dealt with these posts could now destroy them. These afterthoughts meant further raids on income tax and excise offices and a further bag of 100 barracks which brought the total of destroyed barracks to well over 400.

In June there was an attempt on the constabulary post in Edgeworthstown. Its ancient name was Mostrim as is its present name. The barracks was a two-storied building then, in the line of houses which made up the village street. It had a house adjoining it on one side but there was a gap for a laneway on the other side. All of the houses close to the building were of an equal height, and this disposed the post to attack. The barracks was only about five miles from Longford, and this brief distance would make the planning to be extra cautious to prevent reinforcements quickly reaching the village. The 1st and 2nd Longford Battalions were concerned in the attack, but their activity was more in the line of cutting down trees and of making roads impassable than of being close to the barracks.

Connolly and MacEoin had brought a good number of cart boxes with them this time. The intention was to shatter the barracks roof and then drop in some of the cart box bombs inside, but as the men were moving up the village an alarm disturbed them. The 9th Lancers were out in the countryside in the Ardagh direction to the south of the town, and they were moving towards the post to be attacked. It would seem then that the British were aware of what was to happen and that soon they would surround the outposts. Cavalry, however, would have kept to the roads at night as only officers who had hunted over the ground would have had a working knowledge of it. Besides, the clip clop of hooves would give long-distance warning to any of the groups who were the defence for the fellers of trees. A horse at night in close country has, however, one advantage over a man on foot; a horse can run away quicker than a man can run. The outposts were ordered to withdraw, and men returned in disappointment to their area, but the 2nd Battalion men under Commandant Michael Murphy hacked away at their timber for three hours before they found that their neighbours had gone. There was a certain relief later when it was found that the Lancers were not aware of any contemplated attack. They had been carrying out a night exercise in their course of training. Morale would seem to be elastic to put up with these two reverses of Drumlish and Edgeworthstown, but there was no fixed standard of efficiency, training or morale in the IRA. Their standards went and came like the folds in a concertina. They were ready to condone any mistakes made by their officers, and what to regulars might be a defeat to the Volunteers would be a cause of enthusiasm.

Early in June, Connolly was searching around for a barracks to attack. He had questioned Frank Davis about the possibility of Ballinamuck Barracks as a target, but Davis had been brought up around that village, and he knew that the barracks was about one of the strongest in the county. It had two high towers as bastions on two corners diagonally opposite to each other. These were slitted for rifles, and they were each about quarter the size of the barracks, but strangely enough there was no trap door to the roof. There was a fifteen foot wall around the barracks on two sides; on the third side the wall was ten feet higher and in front was a stone wall topped with high railings. The barracks may have been built as a result of the fact that there had been a short fight near the village in 1798.

Connolly went to Ballinamuck on two successive nights with Davis so that he could have an idea of the strength of the cut stone building. When they were some distance from the barracks on the second night, Connolly asked,

'Can you get a good ladder?'

'I can', said Davis for he knew a house which had a strong ladder in the village.

'We can raise the ladder against the ball alley and throw bombs from the top of it on to the roof', said Connolly as they cycled.

Davis knew the ball alley. He had played handball many a time against the wall and he had then climbed on to the barracks roof to recover handballs lost in the valley which was of lead and six feet wide. The ball alley was behind the barracks. It was separated from the barracks wall by a passage, and the wall of the ball alley was 25 feet in height. There was a double roof on the barrack separated by the valley. Connolly saw the weak point in the defence. If the barracks' roof could be broken in, incendiary material could be thrown on to the valley where it could flow down to the inside and then a few cart box bombs could shatter portions of the floor or the walls. Connolly asked to have a strong pump taken from a shop in the town, but a lieutenant from that Ballinamuck Company had accidentally shot one of his own men during the raid and the pump was not taken away. The pump would have been useful as it would have directed a stream of petrol or paraffin from the top of the ladder to the valley. Now, instead of this useful contrivance, men would have to carry bottles filled with an incendiary mixture to the top of the ball alley and from that position hurl them on to the roof valley.

Two battalions, the 1st Battalion under Seán MacEoin and the 5th Battalion under J. J. Brady, had arranged to block the roads leading to Ballinamuck on the night of 9 July. This was the evening of a fair in Longford town, consequently there would be fewer remarks passed on men moving on the roads. When the men, who were to be busy later around the barracks, had come together a mile outside the village, word came that military were in Drumlish a little over four miles away. They had come from Longford and were strengthening the RIC barracks with sandbags and barbed wire.

Connolly sent Frank Davis at once to Drumlish. He was to get what information he could about the strength of the military, and he was to find out exactly what the reinforcements were doing in the village. Until such time as he returned with his report, the attacking party would remain where they were.

Davis found that barbed wire was being festooned around the barracks in such a way that it would now be difficult to come close to it. There were four lorries beside the barracks and the troops had come out from Longford. He waited there for a while close to the barracks then cycled back as hard as he could to Bandra where Connolly was impatiently waiting. The delay had put back the attack by some hours. On this July morning there would be daylight soon after three o'clock. The main danger point now would be from the Drumlish direction. Extra men were sent to strengthen the barricades to the west and extra shotguns and rifles were added to the defence in that direction.

Connolly and MacEoin went to the ball alley. The ladder was hoisted against the wall quietly. Then a cart box was landed on the valley and when it exploded with a shattering roar, it broke the slates and awakened the twelve police. Bottles of paraffin and petrol splashed on to the roof and down through the smashed slates and laths. In a few minutes the roof was on fire and fire spread quickly through the building. The roof supports must have been very old and exceedingly dry. Very lights were shot off at once by the police. They could be seen by the outposts who were out waiting for the soldiers from Drumlish. It was daylight by the time the barracks was on fire, and shortly afterwards flame and smoke poured upwards but there was no answer to the demands for surrender. The swiftness of the blaze had amazed Connolly who had expected that it would take some hours to burn out the post. The police must have made for the outhouses which were backed by the walls of the enclosure, although later it was thought that the RIC were hidden in underground tunnels. Whether they were or not, there was a blazing barracks open to the sky as the roof had fallen further inwards and the heat would keep any intruders at a distance. The high walls were now a protection to the RIC, who, if they were in the outhouses, could beat off any attackers who would have to cross an open space to come close to them. The attack was called off, news was sent to the outposts and the men from the two battalions went cautiously to their homes. That day the police withdrew from what was once their stronghold at Ballinamuck. The sergeant who held the post was made a head constable, and this was a particular honour in Co. Longford which had already two head constables, one in each of the two strong garrisons at Longford and Granard.

Tom Reddington was Longford Brigade Commandant. He was a Galway man who had been a woodwork instructor acting under the Department of Technical Instruction. As a result of his position he was able to go through the county. He held classes in schoolrooms and court houses, and he could always keep in touch with the Volunteers of the neighbourhood. Reddington had been arrested in 1919. When he was being brought to Mountjoy in a lorry, he stooped down because he saw a clip of .303 ammunition on the floor. He handed the clip to the nearest soldier with whom he had been talking. 'Maybe this is of use to you' he said. The soldier became more friendly and before they reached Dublin, he had promised to get grenades out from the Top Barracks in Longford, for money. The brigadier was released when he had served a sentence of three months. When he came back to Longford he met his soldier, whose name was Geordie,[2] and he introduced some of the Volunteers to him. Rifle ammunition and hand grenades were brought out to eager hands outside the barracks, but Geordie soon found that if he wished to increase his earnings, he would have to trust a few of his own soldier comrades. Care had to be taken when ammunition or arms were bought from British soldiers. Some of them would sell for money but others of them would make a bargain by arrangement with their officers. When the Volunteer had kept his appointment and had met his friendly soldiers, he would move away with his booty only to find that he was suddenly surrounded by military in ambush. As a result men in Volunteer companies had lost money, arms and liberty. A man could then get five years hard labour for the possession of arms.

Geordie had been tested by degrees, and he had always carried out his bargains. Suddenly in a check up of supplies, ammunition was missed from a store. A close check was then kept on the arms and ammunition, but some rifles were reported to be missing. Traps were set to catch some of the soldiers who might have been responsible for the disappearance of war material, and as a result in spring of 1920, Geordie and a few Lancer friends of his deserted. They wandered on towards Ballinalee for that name they knew of as a centre. They found friends there. Soon they were working on farms, and they worked well although their pay was mostly through cigarettes and in the money for an odd drink. The Lancers with their methodical army training were serviceable with hunters, and they were satisfied when they had a horse to look after. One of them asked to be sent home to England, but as he was on his way he was picked up in Belfast, and the remainder of his friends decided that Ireland was the safest place for them to work in. Geordie was a good worker on land although he had previously been a Welsh miner. In a way he was a mystery to the IRA men who knew him. He now knew a number of officers and men by sight and by name. There was the danger of his being picked up by a British raiding party, who would have their own brutal methods of getting information about local houses and men from a deserter, but as against that was a chance that he would get additional rifles out of the barracks. The deserters had now to avoid raiding parties but they were both careful and alert. They could now almost smell the approach of danger. When the RIC or military were in their neighbourhood, the Lancers suddenly disappeared for each of them had several hideouts. In a way they were prisoners, watched over by the sons of the house and an eye put on them from time to time by the neighbours. Geordie had talked to Connolly and to MacEoin about the capture of all the rifles in the Top Barracks, but although he was listened to, the suggestion seems to have made the officers suspicious. It was too good to be true they thought, for all the rifles would now be in the guardroom. There was a guard of eight to ten men, a sentry inside the gate and the guardroom was immediately to the left of the gate and about six yards from it. The delay in decision meant a change in the disposition of the rifles. By the time it was decided to risk men being lost on information that might be uncertain or dangerous, the rifle store had been again changed. In the guardroom now were the rifles of the guard secured by a chain which ran through their trigger guards. It was a decision now of the Sybelline books, and the decision was to act at once.

Geordie was a jaunty sparrow of a man who had a girl in Longford town. He went in there frequently to see her and to meet his friends from the Top Barracks, for the loyalty of soldiers to each other was something apart from army discipline, which meant often the geometric progression of harsh authority from sergeants to officers. The men protected themselves and their own delinquencies. They were miserably paid, indifferently fed and most often harshly used. As a result of his meetings in pubs with his Lancer friends, Geordie knew the gossip of the Barracks and the current situation of the men inside.

The risk of the proposed raid had often been talked about, and the men picked for it knew that if anything went wrong they would be trapped. The barracks was comprised of isolated two-storied blocks separated by the gateway. Down from the gate ten foot high walls led down to the roadway fifty yards away. If anything went wrong while the raid was being carried out the men would be trapped in this narrow passage.

The plan was simple enough. Geordie on a September evening at about eight o'clock, when it was dark, walked up to the gate with a parcel under his arm and a revolver in his other hand. Behind him were the picked men who kept close to the dark shelter of the high walls. Geordie kicked the wicket gate as soldiers were accustomed to knock.

'Who's there', the sentry questioned.

'I want to see Sergeant Major Upton', was the reply. 'I have a parcel with me for his wife.'

The sentry listened to the reassuring sound of a Yorkshire voice, and he then opened the wicket. As he opened it Geordie put his foot against it so that it could not be closed.

'You can't see the Sergeant Major', the sentry said.

'Well you'll do', said Geordie as he held up the astonished soldier.

Seán Duffy pulled the sentry outside the gate while the other men rushed into the guardroom. The sergeant of the guard tried to seize a rifle but MacEoin hit him on the head with a revolver. The remainder of the guard quickly put up their hands to order. With a wrench of his powerful hands MacEoin tore away the staples which bedded the chain, then the rifles rattled on to the floor in a heap. Quickly rifles, bayonets and ammunition were carried to the road opening of the walled approach where J. J. Brady, a commercial traveller, and the Commandant of the 5th Battalion, was waiting with his car. Then the men who remained near the guardroom to prevent an alarm being raised came away to the roadway and walked away cheerfully.

Chapter 5

Longford, September 1920
Ballymahon and Arvagh Barracks

———

There had been eight to twelve rifles captured from the Mostrim Barracks on that September evening, but their number varies with different storytellers. Already their immediate use had been discussed. Seán Connolly had gone into the details of a plan for an attack on Ballymahon Barracks on the night after the capture of the rifles in the Top Barracks.

Connolly next morning was out close to Ballymahon where he met some of the South Longford officers. He was arranging with them about roadblocks and obstructions and as well he had to see about explosives and incendiary material. Ballymahon was close to the Westmeath boundary. Due to the destruction of empty barracks there were no small posts nearby, but there were three strong military garrisons within fifteen miles of the village: Longford to the North, Athlone to the Southwest, and to the East some nineteen miles away was Mullingar. Athlone was a British brigade headquarters. There was timber around the village sufficient to add additional tree blocks in case of a protracted resistance. The Longford garrison would know the country best and from that town cavalry might be used in the morning to cut off stragglers.

The Longford Brigade had two drivers whom they could always depend on, Frank Davis and J. J. Brady. Drivers then were very scarce as there were few cars on the road, and as a car was in general the symbol of respectability, it could be surmised that the owner would be either unfriendly or apathetic. The rifles and other weapons were collected by Davis at Seán MacEoin's forge in Kilshrewley. Then MacEoin and Seamus Conway went in the van towards Barry, two miles north of Ballymahon where they met Connolly's outposts. The men were paraded, weapons and ammunition were carefully examined and men were picked to handle the captured rifles which 24 hours previously had been in the Longford guardroom. The officers from the 1st, 3rd, and 4th Battalions, who were to be in charge of the men in outpost positions, moved off to make their own preparations while the van and the motor car went on to the village. As they moved on in the darkness bright flashing lights in the distance, which had at first put them cautiously on the alert, were discovered to be the kerosene lamps belonging to a travelling show which was preparing also for its night's work. The motor vehicles halted near the chapel and could be depended on to remove the wounded or any captured material. Cumann na mBan had a dressing station in the village and in it the girls waited for the attack to begin.

The Ballymahon Barracks was the end house of a terrace of three houses, and as it shared a yard with the house above it, entry had to be made by the back door of the third house. Seán Connolly with a few officers removed the people from this third house to safety. They broke through a fireplace to the house beside the barracks where they smashed the ceiling of the top room to make a hole in the slates. Next, sitting astride the barracks roof the slates were powdered with a sledgehammer until the splinters flew in a dangerous hail. While this preliminary smashing was going on fire was directed obliquely from across the street on to the barracks windows and doors to occupy the minds of the police.

Seamus Conway and Ned Gormley were at the back of the barracks with a sack of GHQ percussion bombs. Conway had been practising with these awkward missiles for some days before the attack, having first removed the striker sets. The grenades carried streamers or feathers to direct their flight and to induce them to land on their detonated end. The danger was that if the arm struck anything behind it while a grenade was being thrown in the dark there would not be much left of the bomber. Conway threw a few of the bombs, but they did not strike by their detonated ends on the sloping roof, for they slid with a clatter to the ground below, but did not explode. Disgusted with their heavy incapacity he flung a few Mills grenades which made sufficient noise to impress the constabulary. In the meantime Connolly had thrown cart box bombs in through the holes in the barracks roof. They exploded with a deafening crack inside in the confined space.

Ballymahon was a strong barracks with stone walls on either side of the passageway. The rooms and passage were pierced with loopholes as if it had been intended that the constabulary would fight from room to room. In the late spring, British army engineers had been sent throughout the country to make RIC barracks secure from attack. Loopholes had been cut on exposed gables and these loopholes had often been lightly plastered up again so that an observer would not be able to detect an aperture. Loopholes in addition were cut in any place where a field of fire was demanded. Windows were protected by steel plates, and by netting wire to deflect grenades or rifle grenades. There were heavy steel doors to guard entrances and exits. The sappers played with barbed wire in a new kind of Celtic interlacement that in festoons and complicated knots would deny to Celtic exuberance the waste spaces which the wire covered. Inside, rooms had been strengthened by sandbags and one room had been made the prototype of the dungeon keep where the final stand was made against the bould invader. The sappers had done their best, and they had created a legend of mined approaches that would have put Uncle Toby[1] off on extra parenthesis, and concealed tunnels and shafts which would have been the envy of a Western eighteenth-century smuggler. In addition there was a pepper sprinkling of Black and Tans, a few with mythical cognomens, but as regards the Black and Tans there I leave you for you now have to raise either your own imagination or the memories of your relatives.

The crashing noise to front and rear had no effect. There was no sign of the RIC moving out to surrender. There was another type of bomb in reserve which had been worked out by Connolly. In those days when snuff was a necessity for old people and the middling old, and when the price was low, the empty tins were plentiful. Now, the refilled tins contained brimstone, flour and gelignite with maybe a sprinkling of red pepper to season and a detonator to encourage its distribution by gelignite. The lid was securely bolted in position. When Connolly had ignited the fuse he held it in his hand until the spitting length had burned itself away somewhat. The effect inside was a mixture of acrid smoke and throat catching fumes which spread through the building. Additional snuff tins scattered added fumes and gas. At last the police had had enough. They may have been expecting the next variation in attack which might be worse than the suffocating smoke which was being billowed against them. They shouted out that they were prepared to surrender.

They handed out their rifles and bayonets, their ammunition, revolvers and egg bombs, their Very light pistols and heavy cartridges. Among the shining weapons was a new defensive protection, which the attackers had heard of, but had not yet seen. It was made of light bullet proof steel in the shape of a waistcoat which was strapped in position on the chest and back. Constabulary officers sometimes used them and some military officers were said to carry them. Police whose names had been reported to IRA Intelligence for the ill treatment of prisoners or the shooting down of civilians and volunteers, and who were aware of their own ill-fame, were partial to their use, as were the remaining detectives of the 'G' Division in Dublin. Some of the lads tried on the waistcoat in turns, and they wondered for what man in the barracks it had been provided. The police were brought down to the church where they faced the wall with their hands up. Although they had been assured of their own lives, some of them showed their nervousness for they were unable to believe that they would be allowed to get away unharmed. Their position as helpless prisoners made them the more uneasy. They were marched across the bridge over the Inny River, locked into a shed and they were told to remain inside.

The surrounding roads had been well blocked by men from the three battalions. On the Edgeworthstown road trees had been practically cut through, then held in position by ropes. On the return journey the van got through but the trees began to sway and only by a determined effort did men swinging from ropes hold back the timber until the car passed under them, when there was a heavy crash in the darkness. Further north a railway crossing had been kept open by a friendly gatekeeper. At night there was then little or no motor traffic on the roads and gates were closed to allow night goods trains to rumble on their way. Next day British reinforcements found the problem of the road blocks difficult. A good deal of timber in the wooded area around the barracks had been dropped and not until afternoon did British troops reach the disarmed garrison. The men were excited by the two successful arms gatherings for 21 good rifles had now been added to the scanty brigade armament.

Before the end of September 1920, simultaneous attacks were planned on four barracks: Granard, Arvagh, Mohill and Ballinamore. Arvagh was in Co. Cavan, Mohill and Ballinamore were in South Leitrim. Seán Connolly was to deal with Ballinamore. It was an isolated post and a strong one. MacEoin with Seamus Conway were to attack Mohill; Seán Duffy was to attempt Granard;

and Pat Finnegan, Arvagh. Concerted action was ruled out by too much talk and information about enemy activity came in before the concerted attacks were to take place. Mohill had been suddenly strengthened with added steel plates and sandbags. Troops were active in and around Ballinamore. Seamus Wrynn, the Brigade Vice Commandant of South Leitrim, brought the information to the Longford men at noon on the day the attacks had been arranged, and as the officers waited additional reports of activity came in from Leitrim. Arvagh was being carefully watched, but nothing unusual had happened there, and it would seem as if the attack on that post could be carried out that night. A few South Leitrim officers, Seamus Wrynn and John Joe O'Reilly, waited on for the attack as they had been deprived of the chance of a fight in their own county.

Arvagh was on the border of the two areas. Men from the 1st and 2nd Longford Battalions from Columcille and Ballinalee were co-operating with Aughnacliffe and Carrigallen Volunteers from South Leitrim. There was a house on either side of the Arvagh Barracks and connected to it by an arched passage. The plan was to get into a house next door to the police, break through the ceiling to the roof, and, as had happened at Ballymahon, smash up a portion of the barracks roof, and then drop in cart box bombs.

Seamus Conway was in the rear with his usual sack of grenades. He was watching the windows until his eyes would become accustomed to the darkness. In front he knew there were angled steel shutters and netting which warded off grenades. Now as his eyes accustomed themselves to the surrounding murk he noticed that a small room jutted out at the back, and to his surprise there was no steel plate on the window. He moved up to within five yards of this annex to find out about the Achilles heel. He could lob in a bomb easily through the window. He threw a Mills grenade in through a window. He heard the sound of falling glass, and as he waited he counted the seconds but there was no further sound beyond the thud of the Mills as it bumped inside on a wooden floor. Even an unexploded grenade was a source of danger to a garrison he knew. It might yet work as a result of delayed action and if any of the garrison had crept down to discover what the noise meant even the sight of a grenade on the floor would probably make the RIC men leave the potential scatterer of cast iron alone where it lay.

Conway threw another Mills grenade, but beyond the bumping noise he might as well have hurled in a few stones. There was something the matter with the grenades. He sent a young lad around to the front to inform Connolly and MacEoin that his grenades were useless, but that there was an unprotected window in the back through which other grenades or cart boxes could be flung. The grenades Connolly was using had been given over to an ex-British soldier who was expected to know about hand grenades. To men unaccustomed to the use of arms a trained soldier was expected to know weapons upside down and responsibility, which was easy enough to delegate, could be imposed upon another because he had served in foreign parts. Evidently that was specialised work in the British army. Always there was a certain dread of grenades by men who had never previously used them or who had not had their mechanism carefully explained. Sometimes they had been thrown into action with the pins in position. A nervous man was only too willing to get rid of their unwelcome weight, and on a few occasions striking sets, which should have been kept separate, had not been inserted. The grenades had been stored in the Columcille area, and Conway had been told they were ready for use. As he stripped a grenade he found that it did not contain its striking set, and as he handled the remainder in the darkness, found that they were all ignorant of sets. He cursed his own lack of thought in not having first examined some of the missiles before he had gone to the back of the barracks. He had, however, a light cart box, a donkey cart box. He heaved it through the window and beyond the succession of bumps he heard a loud crash which was intensified by the darkness and by his former disappointments.

In the meantime Connolly and other men had been breaking through the fireplace on the first floor with the intention of using a heavy cart box which had an ample supply of gelignite. The men used crowbars and picks. In a short time there was a gaping hole. Connolly lit the fuse, slung in the charge, but unknown to him the archway was a blanket of air in between the fireplace and the barracks. The cart box dropped to the ground but it made up for in noise for what it now lacked in effectiveness. There was a shattering crash. The sound might echo well, it could only achieve damage in sound. He shouted to the police to surrender. Suddenly a figure rushed out of the front door and crossed the street. In the darkness the dark uniform was not observed, but the sound of heavy boots echoed up and down the street. Then a voice came from an archway opposite to the post: 'I'm sergeant . . . I surrender the barracks.' The voice continued to command the police inside, but it was interrupted by their rifle fire; after a while the RIC came out with their rifles.

Seán Connolly handed the prisoners over to Frank Davis, who brought them into Elliots next door to their barracks, and while he looked after the police, the barracks was buzzing as a swarming hive with men rushing for ammunition and equipment. This was always a doubtful garnishing as clips of rifle ammunition, stray grenades and a revolver might quickly find an aching pocket, especially when more than one battalion was concerned in an operation. Here there were men from three battalions, and there were two brigades concerned for the night's treasure trove.

While Davis was searching the prisoners for papers or notebooks, he saw a policeman fall suddenly on the floor. He thought the man had fallen in a fit, and as he stooped to help him, he saw he was a Tyrone constable named Brennan who had once served in Ballinamuck. He knew Davis, and Davis knew him, and now the policeman was in dread. Davis sent for Seán Connolly who was checking the captured police armament, and when Seán came into Elliots, Davis told him the story of the fearful constable.

In 1919 Davis had been a lieutenant in the Ballinamuck Company. Coming home from parade one night with a few men they walked through the village, and as they walked they broke out in song:

> It's a wrong thing to fight for England
> It's a wrong thing to do
> It's a wrong thing to fight for England
> Who murdered our brave and true

From a dark corner of the street waiting police had listened to the voices and the words, neither of which they seemed to like. As the men came close to them the police jumped out, grabbed Davis by the arms and the remainder of the chorus disappeared into the sheltering darkness. They led their prisoner towards the barracks, but he stopped suddenly, forked his legs, tripped up his custodians and jumped over their fallen bodies. Brennan had threatened that the next time he had a sight of Davis he would shoot him, and when he had Davis in view now the sight of him was both unexpected and unpleasant.

Seán Connolly pulled Brennan up from the floor.

'What's the matter with you?' he asked.

'Davis will surely shoot me now', the policeman said, 'and I don't want to be shot.'

'We'll soon settle that', said Connolly.

He found a sheet of writing paper in the room and he wrote for a while. Then he showed what he had written to the RIC man. Brennan, it stated, would not remember the names of any of the men present that night nor would he identify any of them if they were captured subsequently. He was never again to come into Co. Longford, and if he came into the county, he was liable to be shot. Brennan was ready to sign the paper, but Connolly said crisply 'Oh wait a minute I must have a bible before we are finished with you.' The police looked curiously and some apprehensively at this ceremonious approach towards one of themselves who had been too exuberant. Each of them had examined his own police record for any memory of his open hostility when Connolly came into the room. Even in 'The Force' there were walls within walls of secret spyings like these wooden Chinese eggs which fit into one another until the ultimate core is hardly visible. The elderly police were in a decided difficulty about their future. Some had a few years to go until they could retire on pension and their loyalty was somewhat divided between this monetary security for age, their personal survival if they continued in the RIC, and their resentment at living under active service conditions, backed by military whom they had no particular wish for, and comraded by Tans for whom they had contempt save when they were under fire together. Seán MacEoin searched for a bible. Ordinarily a bible might be found in an occasional Catholic house, and its purpose would be mainly to record the dates of birth of the parents and the children of that house. This, however, was a Protestant house, and a bible was soon found. Brennan was put on his knees. He repeated the words Connolly read out to him, then he swore he would keep his oath, and finally he signed the paper.

'You'd best keep your oath', said Connolly.

The constable stayed outside of the county from that date and the only time he was known to have entered it was to visit his old station in Ballinamuck. Then he lay down on the floor of the lorry and kept to the floor while his companions were in the neighbourhood.

The sergeant was worried about the barracks which was very little damaged. He asked that it be burned so that he and his companions could prove that they had defended their post. Connolly would anyhow have burned the barracks, but it was as well to please the sergeant who had saved his men, unexploded grenades and ammunition. When the barracks was on fire, another small area was freed from the immediate menace of the RIC as an intelligence machine, which watched the movements of suspects, helped to pilot the soldiery, Tans and Auxiliaries on raids and shootings, made use of Loyalists as an auxiliary, gathered rumour and gossip from every pragmatic contact, spread whatever venom-tipped rumour as would discredit local republicans and strained their collars to track down real fighting men and the dangerous non-fighting men of their areas. With them too went the undue sense of their own importance, which, apart from their useful continuous prying, was always multiplied by them for their authorities, and with them too went British prestige as a support to those openly or passively hostile to the Republic and to its institutions. The RIC were now only the symbol of a force which was once responsible for law and order, and which now held their blockhouses on the defensive. They were yet the antennae of the military. They knew the town and countryside inside and out; they knew the people. Without them few raids could take place, fewer prisoners could be identified, and the military machine would be left to strike ruthlessly and blindly.

The ten captured rifles, revolvers, ammunition and egg bombs were put into the waiting cars. There were two heavy boxes which were securely locked. The men wondered what was in them and as they bent under their wonderful weight they were pleased for they must be a load of heavy bombs, or new kinds of weapons. The blocking parties had again cut the roads, had thrown down stone walls at intervals or had felled timber where there were demesnes or plantations. In this way men of the companies on outpost duty with shotguns, or working with picks, shovels and cross cuts were helping the main attack which could not have been carried through without the security which they gave. Again the Very lights of the garrison had brought no help. Imperial help was near but it was far enough away when it was needed in the darkness.

On the way from Aughnacliffe to Ballinalee twenty men were used to push the car up some of the hills for the mighty treasure asserted its strength. Next morning, Davis who was quartermaster smashed in the heavy boxes and then there was a long silence as heavy as the contents. Not bombs, nor even a new kind of weapon met his astonished gaze, but the official weights and measures of the Cavan City Council with which other weights and measures had to be equated.

MacEoin and Conway stayed in the village that morning secure in their knowledge of the road blocking zeal of the two brigades. They went to Mass there but no relief force made their way to the RIC. Not until Tuesday did a strong column of military and police cut their way into the district. Longford, up to mid-September 1920, was lacking in one respect and that was that punitive expeditions had not yet begun to burn or destroy houses, shops and creameries. In North Tipperary and Mid Tipperary, in Kerry and in other areas burnings, lootings and reprisals made the capture of a post or the success of an ambush to smart sorely on the people in the neighbourhood. Not until November did Longford houses suffer for the activities of its men. The brigade had now a pride in its efforts during this month when over thirty good enemy rifles were ready to be used against the British.

Chapter 6

North Roscommon, October 1920
Castlenode

———————

Seán Connolly had helped to start an activity in his native county, ably helped by a band of resolute men and backed by areas such as Columcille and Clonfin, where the people were their strength, security and the second line of defence. Now in October 1920, he was summoned to GHQ where he met some of the Staff, particularly Diarmuid O'Hegarty and Eamonn Price who were concerned with organisation, and Michael Collins and Richard Mulcahy who had various interests. In North Roscommon there was a feeling of unrest, and it was decided that Connolly should go there. There were men who wanted to attempt operations but the brigadier, Seamus Ryan, seemed to be in the way. He was a friend of Collins and had been a long time in the movement, but he was inclined to solve problems by leaving them alone. In such areas when men were held up unduly from activity, the British would hold the upper hand, and continue to make their authority heavily felt when any small action succeeded. The British method was to cow and browbeat if a brigade was ineffective or unwilling to fight.

Before Connolly went on to Roscommon, however, he visited battalion areas in his own Longford Brigade. He saw the companies were working at their own routine and that training was at as systematic a standard as its unprofessional teachers could reach. Usually he, as the brigade vice-commandant, was responsible for the special services such as intelligence, engineering, first aid and others, and it was part of his duty to organise these special departments and to see that they were not only on a working basis, but on a fighting basis. Weakness generally lay in intelligence, engineering and signalling. Operations could not be effectively carried out without the first two, and security often depended upon the third. The brigade vice-commandant was really an organiser if he devoted his planned time to his area. Although it was October, flying columns, which had been organised in some brigades in Munster, had not yet begun in Leinster or in Connaught. The efficiency of a column would depend upon the development of organisation in a brigade. If battalions were virile and alert and had their special services working well and had already some experience of action, then a column would find work ready for it in each battalion which it visited. Connolly had spent a good deal of his time in planning operations, some of which had been turned into action. That was the realistic method of developing a morale which would give an impetus in increasing the interest of the men in the real organisation of their units.

As an organiser Seán Connolly would have to possess a detached attitude even to his own brigade. Wherever he went now would be his own new area, but he would find that he would have to build up the trust and confidence of the new unit in himself. He would now have to make decisions regardless of what following some inefficient officers had, or he might have to act against the current judgement of a battalion, who were obstinate out of false loyalty. The local system of minor chiefs being cocks in their own dunghill persisted in many counties, but the authority of Dáil Éireann was yet a very real authority which was invariably obeyed by those who gave allegiance. Procrastination, carelessness and irresoluteness made holes in the fabric of allegiance, but beyond the weakness of evasion and misplaced cunning there would be no deliberate disloyalty. However inefficient men were in their training or in their will to action, they had long distance discipline of desire. In an area which had not yet begun to fight, an organiser could create his own legend quickly by his driving efforts to plan and to take part in action, although his mythos would drop beyond the mists of local memory if other men from the area carried on a similar pressure against the enemy when he had gone away.

Connolly had been brought up with men who had later become his Volunteer comrades in Longford. The depths and strengths of country knowledge of a background which, through lack of a critical historical tradition was rapidly becoming more personal in relationships, bound the parish together. By personal experience he knew of safe places to sleep, men to trust, or he could rely on his friends for knowledge that was outside his own experience. He would know a large circle of people because he happened to be born in their district, and the roots and branches of his degrees of relationship would extend his knowledge. Now he had to judge a man by a swift meeting, or by casual talk or by directed question at a battalion council. He had to learn judgment of voice, appearance, gesture by inconsequential things which he would brood on later, instead of being guided by deep-rooted knowledge. Local jealousy of a man from a neighbouring county could flare up at times, and some of the older men might swallow their suspicion hard, but the time was welding a unity of purpose which would accept a unity of discipline as the fight went on. An area would quickly serve a good man who tested them in action. If he was willing to take risks, they were usually willing to follow no matter how poor a confidence they had in themselves.

In a middling area where organisation was slack and officers somewhat lackadaisical, though well meaning, he would find it difficult to get orders carried out either accurately or promptly. If he wished to remedy the inherited system of improvisation and replace it by careful thought and insistent practice, he would have to take his time.

In a boggy district a road is built on a floating foundation of brushwood, and of light material which makes a springboard surface for the imposition of heavier metal. If weight goes first on a bog, then a switchback surface results like a succession of horses ridden too young. In a bog area of the mind the same principle had to be observed to avoid the undeveloped will and the slough of despond of a leaderless unit. This he knew. He was aware that the determination to continue wherever the road led was as important as the decision to take on the responsibility for action. The foundation had to be laid lightly first.

The legend of Connolly's ease of manner was well known. If he got angry, he could conceal his anger; if he had to wait, he showed patience. There is a memory of gentleness in difficulties and of a determination to get things done, of suffering disappointments and reverses, yet of going on again against difficulties. As a test of his continued influence, there is a failure in the two areas he worked in to continue the fight, but as a legend he survives. But then Seán Connolly is dead, and it is easier to judge the dead when the period he is accessed by is an intensive period of a few years. A man should be judged by his mentality, by his awareness, by his mixture of the good and the bad, and of his growth or lack of growth in consciousness and by other standards as difficult to assess. A man who survives a period of intensity which happened to be action, if he lives is judged also by the here and now. The dead are often, strangely enough, opaque in their amber.

In North Roscommon, Connolly spent a good deal of his time around Ballinamore parish which had a good company, although untried. The brigadier, Seamus Ryan, also made use of this area. Connolly and he could resolve their doubts of each other by making music together, for the brigadier was partial to a melodeon and

Connolly's fingers itched for a fiddle. They could then ease their situations in accord. Some of the North Roscommon officers had been anxious to fight, to begin somewhere or somehow, but they were restrained. One of them had been severely censured for giving a Volunteer, who was one of a number who wished to join the RIC, a charge of shot in the behind at a long distance. A few of these Volunteers did join the RIC, but were kept away from their county for their own safety. Headquarters listened to their difficulties, but the brigadier, Ryan, had been long in the movement and the chief-of-staff, Richard Mulcahy, did not wish to remove him. At the end of October, however, some of the officers were told that Seán Connolly would be sent down to help, by being responsible himself for whatever activity would develop as a result of his presence in the area.

Boyle, about six miles away from Ballinamore, had a strong military barracks. The soldiers were housed in what had once been the town house of Lord Lorton. It had then fronted the old road to Carrick and the river Boyle. Now, the barracks with its added buildings had its back to the river. The RIC had a strong garrison close to the military barracks, and there was an Auxiliary company in the asylum which raided at random throughout the neighbouring counties. Boyle was an old garrison town whose barracks had for hundreds of years been in the fine Cistercian Abbey which, as was usual with that reticent order, made the aesthetics of decoration straight laced, with little of decoration left behind it in Boyle save a number of simply but beautifully carved capitals. Boyle Barracks had about six cells in the dark basement of the buildings which had been detention cells for British delinquents. No decent quarters were provided for the prisoners who were becoming numerous. Indeed, after a few escapes captives were confined without exercise in deliberately unsanitary conditions until a bad outbreak of typhoid forced the military to send them to Mountjoy. The town had few friendly people in it and what few there were bore the yoke which enemy and townspeople pressed down hard. Volunteers in such garrison towns had to clear out as soon as fighting began, but the few Republicans left behind had to put up with the drunken Tans who were capricious in their belabourings and Auxiliaries who could be half savage and half sporting as the mood took them. The Auxiliary commander was able to keep his company in check, but they needed watching. Patrick Delahunty, the North Roscommon Brigade Intelligence Officer who lived in the town, could occasionally obtain information from the District Inspector. He, as a head constable, had been responsible for Roger Casement's arrest. Some of the other constables and a sergeant, who had been similarly employed then, had been shot off, possibly by Collins's orders. The District Inspector had gone, it is said, to make his peace with Collins in person. What information he then passed on to GHQ is not now known locally, but a few times he sent out warnings about an impending raid. The brigadier had, as well, a friendly constable in Strokestown, a District Inspector's clerk, who gave information to him and to himself only. This reservation was a safeguard to avoid unnecessary talk, for a District Inspector's clerk was a valuable asset. He would have access to secret papers, and to codes, but to the battalion commandant who was anxious to fight, no information which would be of help to him came through from either of the sharers of information.

When Connolly had visited battalion councils in the four battalions and had seen what organisation there was by question and observation, he formed another battalion out of the 4th Battalion which had run from Hillstreet to the Leitrim and Sligo borders. He had a good look at all the posts which were held in the area. The RIC barracks had been reduced since Easter 1920 by burnings. Along the Shannon the British held the bridgeheads at Lanesborough, which was in the Longford area, Tarmonbarry,

Roosky and Carrick-on-Shannon which was the Leitrim county centre for police and military, but their forces could also be used to snoop into adjacent parts of Roscommon. Keadue in the now 5th Battalion had an RIC garrison and Lord (John) French's occasional residence, Rockingham House, had a garrison, while towards the bounds of the brigade there were barracks in Strokestown, police in Elphin and in Frenchpark. Keadue was isolated, and when he visited the neighbourhood Connolly had an idea that it might be captured, but he intended to wait until he had a few men who had been under fire and until he captured or was given arms.

The brigade was poorly armed. Bill Doherty, the Strokestown company commandant, had been able to buy some arms at GHQ at the end of October; a few rifles had been obtained from deserters in Strokestown as well, but there were few other serviceable weapons. Boyle had a rifle which had been taken from a soldier in the town, but now its bolt was missing and it could only be a curio for which a man could get a good sentence if it was caught in his house. Connolly saw that he would have to rely on mines and/or grenades, which he could help to make, but he thought he might be able to borrow rifles from his own brigade to stiffen the improvised weapons.

Pat Madden from South Roscommon was in need of a motor car. He had been offered arms by GHQ if he could bring them away, and it was then decided to look for a car on the boundaries of his area. A landlord with whom there had been trouble the previous year, William Walpole of Castlenode, had a good car in his garage. The people had driven off his cattle hoping to persuade him to break up his land, but the military, Lancers and footmen had helped to round up the roving beasts, and they had been driven back to their good grazing ground behind a shield of khaki bayonets and lances. The next operation was organised by Volunteers who bared the land of cattle which they drove from company area to company area all through the night and during the following day. Some drivers reached two adjacent counties and a number of large bullocks were never seen again. A bullock with a Republican flag on his strong horns was driven up the drive towards the house as a colour bearer. That *Tain*, reminiscent of earlier forays, made Walpole decide that grass land was not a profitable or an easy way of life, and his estate, later broken up, helped to produce fine crops of potatoes for the Roscommon and Longford markets.

Cattle driving had been strictly forbidden by General Headquarters. It was thought that the reality of land hunger might divert the concentrated attack which was to slowly develop against the British, and that men satisfied with possession would no longer fight dispassionately. In many districts Volunteer companies had prevented cattle being moved from demesne lands by their friends and neighbours, or had enforced the rounding up and the return of the beasts. Here, however, under the shadow of Slieve Bawn, the people were backed by the Volunteers, and they who were already staunch had reason to be more grateful and for once the balance of aid was on the side of the Volunteers.

The Walpole house was in the Strokestown Battalion area where the commandant, Bill Doherty, was able to drive a car. That itself at the time was a distinction. He brought a mechanic with him, but Pat Madden brought men and rifles from Ballagh Company. Two riflemen were placed in a grove of trees near the entrance gate, while the South Roscommon men went up towards the house which was a half a mile away. Old William Walpole came to the door when his presence was asked for: 'I won't give you the car', he said 'but you can take it away if you are able.' Doherty and the mechanic tried to start the engine, but the engine was as hostile as the owner. As is usual in the country where advice on any form of disease or of conduct is always proffered, Doherty and the mechanic now listened to a spate of suggestions from men who had never driven a car. There was only one way of moving the car, it was thought, after a continuous diagnosis of its viscera, and that was by manpower.

The garage was behind the house but only about 25 yards away. Walpole, who was comforted with the failure of the vehicle was nervous and upset. He advised the men to leave the place, and when he saw that they had no intention of leaving, he fell down suddenly in a faint. A short while afterwards the toiling mechanics and the advisory onlookers heard shots in the distance, then the shouting of strange voices and a further spatter of rifle shots across the level demesne. As they rushed out of the garage they could see movement in the distance for the moon was up, and figure blurs came and went as rosy spots of rifle fire were replaced by steady volley firing. Military or police must be near the entrance gate Madden thought, and it looked as if their sentries had been captured or shot.

At the time there were the 9th Lancers in Strokestown Park House which was over a mile and three quarters away from Walpole and there were Tans in the barracks as a reinforcement. The officers had often come out to Walpole to visit and to drink, and they knew their way across country. Pat Madden, Luke Duffy and the South Roscommon men went to the back of the house and by circling around they reached the main road where they sat down to talk. What had happened to the two sentries and what strength of enemy had come along the avenue were questions which they asked themselves but which none of them could answer. The only solution to their uncertainty was to go as far as the grove of trees at the entrance gate and see if they could find out any trace of what had happened to their men. The moon had fallen lower in the sky as they went cautiously back to the plantation. Only a few of them had small arms, but by spreading out in length they decreased the risk of surprise. In among the young trees they found empty rifle cartridges, but although they searched as well as darkness would allow,

there was no sign of what they had been expecting to discover —
dead or wounded men; nor did they find their rifles.

As they stood there they again discussed the strange flame
flickers of rifle flashes which they had first observed. Evidently the
military had come across by the roads from their strong building
and they had by this returned to it. As they looked across the
darkness towards the house, there was no light to be seen and the
only sound was that of cattle munching on what had been left of
the sweet aftergrass. Pat Madden said, 'Everything is quiet now so
we'd best go back and take another turn out of the old car.' Doherty
and the mechanic thought that if a part had been removed, it would
probably be replaced as the householder would never expect the
IRA, after the volleys and their retreat, to return again that night.
This time they crossed the demesne more cautiously. Every few
hundred yards they stopped to listen in the darkness, but nothing
could be heard from the house. Doherty went around to the garage,
but the remainder of the men saw a car on the gravel near the
avenue railings and some of them were able to start the engine. The
men gathered around, pleased, for this new gift was unexpected
and here was a car to replace the other.

The engine noise was quickly put in the shade of quietness by a
sudden blaze of fire from the windows of the house, while the men
behind the weapons cursed them. Bullets buzzed around, but there
was no cover save the thick darkness. The men lay down but no one
fired back as their flashes would only serve as a direction guide to
the men now inside Castlenode. The ambush party inside must
have been waiting patiently for a long time. The South Roscommon
men had scattered, but snipe whistles brought the strangers
together again for none of them knew this country well save Luke
Duffy who had probably shot over it. When they were out of range
of fire from the house, they could yet hear the defenders busily
repulsing an attack which had been concentrated in the sound of

the car engine. Doherty was now not to be found for he had not
been seen since he had gone towards the garage. His disappearance
meant the loss of three men during this strange night operation in
which they failed to take a car, yet luckily none of the men who
remained were wounded.

Next morning Doherty turned up in a long frieze coat and a
bowler hat, driven in a pony trap. He had begun to examine the car
in the garage when bullets came through the door and clanged
against the car metal. Doherty kept close to the wall to avoid
ricochet bullets, but the firing continued for a long time. Then
during a lull in the defence he ran through the door, and as he knew
the country, he was able to get to a friendly house in the murk. A
short time after his arrival news came from Ballagh about the
riflemen. They had heard men crossing the demesne, and when
they spoke their English voices declared them. Realising the
danger their main body was now in, the sentries fired, moved their
positions so as to make it appear they were numerous, and kept
firing. The British threw themselves down for steady shooting.
They blazed along the edge of the wood which they could see as a
blur against the sky, until they felt they had silenced the body of
men who had attacked them.

Evidently Walpole had sent some one of his household on a
hunter horse across country to Strokestown Park House for help.
The Lancers had brought some RIC and Tans with them. The
mixed force had remained in the house to protect the owner and
themselves having been both defenders and attackers themselves.
With the morning light they went back to their posts. Doherty
wanted to have Walpole arrested so that he could be court-
martialled for giving information which endangered their lives, but
the South Roscommon men were against that course. No one had
been either wounded or captured as a result of his information, and
as he was a Protestant, it might look to be a religious reprisal as the

people would not know of the real circumstances. The result of the strange argument was that Walpole was not interfered with and Madden had to go back to his area without a good car.

Connolly had laughed when he heard of the difficulties of trying to capture a motor car. Later when he met the South Roscommon men, he was thinking of an attack on Lanesborough Barracks which would need co-operation with Longford and with the North Roscommon men. He was brought close to Kilteevan to be shown a dugout. It was a makeshift improvisation, unsafe, uncomfortable and awkward for whoever would use it.

'Now what do you think of it?' he was asked with pride.

Connolly laughed: 'It's like a place a bitch would pick on to hide her litter', he said.

Chapter 7

North Roscommon, November–December 1920
Elphin and Ballinalee Barracks

———————

A flying column had been formed in Longford on 1 November 1920. Information had come through from GHQ that there would be general raids on that day and that officers and men should keep out of the way. Yet some of them were arrested. The flying column men had been in action a few days later when Granard and Ballinalee were to have been defended against reprisal parties which were expected to make an onslaught. RIC District Inspector, Philip Kelleher,[1] had been shot dead in Granard on that same day, and on the next day, 2 November, a policeman who had been slowly collecting information for months had been killed. Cooney was his name. He had gone through the Midland counties carefully, frequently changing his clothes so as to slightly change his appearance, and sometimes he was dressed as a woman. Evidently he had not been noticed at his work, and thus GHQ could not inform the brigade of his presence in their command. He had once served as a constable in Ballinalee Barracks, and he was now a mixture of a policeman and a special agent. The fact that he could move around unnoticed was peculiar, as in good areas strangers were quickly noticed by the people if not by the Volunteers. When word about him came from Dublin he was actually close to Ballinalee, but he seemed to disappear. Next day, however, he was found cycling on his bicycle. He carried his information behind the saddlebag in a small leather case, but although the Longford code breakers tried to puzzle out his code, they were unable to extract the information. His notebooks were sent on to the Intelligence branch at GHQ and when they had been worked on, it was found that he had notes on some of the most important men in a few brigades, had watched the houses in which they had stayed and knew about some of the safe houses for volunteers in three counties.

Granard had not been defended as instructed. It had been burned and looted. On their way back to Longford the raiding mixture of Tans and RIC in seven lorries had been badly mauled in Ballinalee which they had come to burn. The column was now under arms there and all their rifles were needed to again defend the village.

Seán Connolly sent Jack Clancy from Drumlion, who was the Adjutant of the 4th Longford Battalion, to Dublin, and as a result of his visit an electric detonator, cable, exploders and explosives were bought there. A telegram was sent to Jim Feely of Boyle, the monumental mason, to tell him that marble was being forwarded to him on a certain day. The 'marble' was met at Drumsna station. It was soon in Ballinameen where it was made use of. Connolly had hoped for a larger donation of explosives and for rifles. He sent Feely to Dublin before Christmas. He had a hundred pounds in notes with him. He met Gearoid O'Sullivan and Piaras Beasley in Vaughan's Hotel, and he had just received a receipt for the money in Gearoid's very legible hand when Christy the Boots came in and told them to get out at once as a raiding party were on their way. O'Sullivan and Beasley handed over documents to the barmaid who quickly put them in a hiding place. The notes were bundled into a large cigarette box for safety, as a till or a safe was then anything but secure from a raiding party. When Feely was close to the Rotunda Hospital he saw three tenders of Auxiliaries coming swiftly from down town. Men were dropped to cover off the approaches before the hotel was raided. Vaughan's was continually being visited by members of the Headquarters Staff and their Intelligence Branch, and it was as continually being raided. Many country officers came here to make an appointment through Christy or to meet GHQ directors. Christy had been arrested shortly before this on suspicion, was brought to the Castle and threatened, then offered a good bribe and here he was again, a complete Intelligence unit in himself receiving information while a raiding party of Auxiliaries were already on their way from Dublin Castle.

North Roscommon Brigade had a hilly area towards the Curlews, to the North of Boyle, and North East towards Kilronan mountain and Geltannasaggart, but the remainder of the Brigade area was rolling grassland, much more suitable for fattening strong bullocks, and for putting bone on sheep which resembled calves in the poor Mayo county to the westward, than for preparing ambushes. There were no clumps of trees, and few hedges even to break the monotony of uneventful view. From Strokestown a few hills hid the low land toward Drumsna which was broken up by connected lakes and many small streams, while the continuation of upland from Slieve Bawn shut off the bogs and callow land towards the Shannon. The winters were more severe in these northern stretches then they were on the eastern side of the Shannon. Snow lingered, frost bit deeply into earth sluggish in drainage and cold dampness was felt in the bones. Rathcrughan, at the eastern edge had a commanding view from the earthworks where Medb and Ailill had had their disastrous pillow-talk,[2] and from near where Medb met the magicians and poets to have her fortune for the year to come told at Samhain.[3] There too before the great *Tain*, Fergus, the exile, interrupted in his game of chess by a thrusting remark of Bricrin had suddenly hit him with a fist which held captured chessmen. The chessmen had remained in the venomous skull to emphasise the Ulsterman's anger.

The long vista, which was useful for royalty to gaze on their herds and horses, made it difficult for men to hold a position for any length of time, and it was unsafe to retreat across when followed up by long-ranged weapons. Only trained riflemen could survive in action here. Connolly knew that it was best to use his strength against police or military patrols or against posts. Patrols south of Ballinameen could be a mixture of Auxiliaries and RIC or of Auxiliaries and military at least fifty strong, but local patrols which came out from protected posts to the south and east were smaller. By late 1920 the British had learned that stereotype formation or movement was inadvisable. Always they felt the piercing eye directed on all their activities from porter drinking to love making, through their letters home and into the security of their steel shutters. They could be met on the roads in lorries well strung out or in foot or cycle patrols which covered a good stretch of ground.

The District Inspector in Boyle was a peaceful man, it is said. He did not want trouble. 'Mary Gorman' he was known as locally, for Mary had been the girl who had given information about Roger Casement's presence on the strand at Banna in Co Kerry. Her nemesis was to serve as a prostitute in London. Now word came through the Director of Intelligence, who had a means of communication in the parish priest that there was to be a raid on Ballinameen in a few days' time. Connolly who was busy at Jack Roche's left the parish with some of the men, and they returned when the raiding party had left the district.

In between inspections Connolly was busy making mines and in getting mines made at Ballinameen. Jack Roche was a good blacksmith, and Michael Roche had a knowledge of the trade. Connolly often stayed at Roche's where both men helped at the forge in making plates and bolts for the cart box grenades which Connolly had to improvise when there were no other available grenades for use. He had a factory at Bessy Kelly's in an unused two-storeyed house which now belonged to Tommy Grady, but it was always spoken of as Bessy's. It was in some hundred yards off the road and was not suspected of harbouring men.

It had been used as a barracks for prisoners when they had been taken away by Republican police to the security of an 'unknown destination'. There was a defensive peculiarity about Bessy's place. It was haunted. When three ex-soldiers had been arrested for stealing cattle and horses, it was to this strong house they had been brought. Noises were heard on the roof and underneath the ground floor, and as they were not occasioned by rats, it was hard to tell whether the ex-soldiers or their guards were more afraid of the strange movements which none of them could explain. 'If it was a ghost', it was a local ghost and that was closer to the Volunteers of the parish than to ex-soldiers who did not belong. Also there was a matter of Volunteer pride which would help untrained men to confront more than the trained courage which had torn up a number of its local roots. The noises helped to act as extra sentries on the prison, but the men soon got bored with keeping watch continually, for there was nothing of the jailer in their nature. Tired of this continual watch the officers sent the cattle thieves to Longford in the nature of a white elephant gift. The Longford men did not favour this continuity of guards for they soon gave the ex-soldiers their return fare to Boyle. Although the RIC tried to get information out of these by a mixture of threats and offers of money, the prisoners refused to give any information either about their captors or their prisons.

The haunting of Bessy Kelly's was useful in its own way. It would keep prowling people away. Ass and horsecart boxes were collected all over the battalion area. Here, they were bored with a drill given to them by MacHenry, a creamery manager in Crughan. The hole led into the explosives and it could be detonated by fuse or by electricity. There were three kinds of these cart box mines or bombs prepared. The horsecart bomb weighed eleven pounds and the asscart bomb seven pounds. They could be used in barracks attacks or against patrols but there was a special mine which Connolly prepared and which he meant to use on patrols. It was a contact mine which would explode when it fell from a height. It was held by a cord and when the cord was jerked the mine fell down.

Seán Connolly had tested one of these mines on the roadside near Mantua. He had placed it on the branches of a tree overhead the road, and hardly was it in position when the twine which was held by Kelly of Rathcrughan gave way. The mine tumbled down and exploded with a shattering burst of scrap metal on all sides. The men who had been brought along to watch the experiment had barely time to duck down behind the wall behind which they stood. The demonstration satisfied Connolly that the mines would explode when they hit the ground, and it more than satisfied the onlookers who had been close to being the experimental guinea pigs as well as observers.

Connolly must have known from the nature of the country that attacks on patrols would have to be carried on in towns and in villages and at nighttime. Night work should have meant shotguns and grenades which are both effective at close range. The use of a rifle at night is a matter of instinct and training and benefits offensive morale by the surprise of shock. On dark nights when the sound of movement is the only target, a revolver is as useful at close range. A shotgun is more surely a question of instinctive use and its spread of charge is more effective.

They had about 30 mines made. In addition, cement mines encased in wood, and which varied in weight from 50 to 85 pounds, had been prepared for use against barracks walls. A two-pound treacle tin filled with gelignite was placed to one side of the concrete and that blast would be more effective against a wall which would be closest to the tin. There were two detonators, one into which the fuse was crimped, the other was electric with wires attached. In case of a failure of one detonator, there was now an alternative one for reuse. They had been sealed with pitch to protect them from dampness but were awkward for moving around with.

Connolly brought men towards Frenchpark, where a patrol of eight RIC police were in the habit of moving out the roads. He had some of the contact mines with him, but although they waited in the freezing air, no police stirred out. Next night he brought men to the dispensary which was on a road fork in the Strokestown direction, about a half mile from Elphin. There was a patrol of from ten to twelve police which moved up and down the town. Sometimes it went out on the roads or it might turn into a pub to drink. The problem was now, as Connolly saw it, whether this patrol could be drawn into a position where the IRA were in waiting for them. If they waited on chance on a different road nights in succession they might be noticed and a chance or deliberate word would put the police on guard ready to be in ambush themselves. Two young lads were to be used as a decoy. They went first into a pub where words were thrown in a provocative manner, and they left the lighted shelter to settle their difference outside. On the street they shouted at each other in the usual sparring way of word play, but soon they were tussling and aiming blows at one another, some of which were hard enough to make the deception realistic. At last the RIC attracted by the shouting came down the street as a patrol. The two lads slowly retreated to the crossroad to Strokestown and as slowly went down the hill.

There was snow on the ground and the air was crackling with frost. The ambush party at the Dispensary had been waiting a long time. They rubbed their hands together and dug them into their pockets for warmth. Nobody, as was customary in the countryside, wore gloves. They heard the shouting voices and terms of abuse coming closer. When the two lads were beside the Dispensary, they dropped quietly into darkness. The two contact mines were on the top of two gateposts and as the patrol crunched by on the frozen snow the strings were pulled. The mines fell down on to two flat stones which had been placed beneath them to make sure that the striking mechanism would fall on a hard surface. The signal to begin the attack was the mine explosions, but the only sounds listening ears heard were two sharp crashes as the cart boxes fell on to the waiting stones. Connolly at once threw a box grenade, and Bill Doherty who had pulled the box strings from a discreet distance away, now threw hand grenades. The RIC cracked away at revolver flashes in the darkness, and the men waited for the next flash to locate individual positions. Both sides retreated in opposite directions. The police went up the hilly ground across the fields to the protection of the town, crackling the frosty air with intensive fire as they hurried to their barracks. The high ground backed their warm flashes. The mines were discovered by the RIC later and their discovery meant that a serious attempt had been made with a formidable weapon on their peaceful occupation at Elphin. As there was no information from the police as to why the mines failed, Connolly was inclined to think that they might have landed on their sides when the striking pins would not work.

The failure of the mines was as disturbing to Seán Connolly as it was upsetting to the men. It had been their first fight. They had been nervously eager to do their best and the mines upon which they had depended most for success had failed them. It was said that some of the police had been wounded, but that was small satisfaction as compared with the doubt which had replaced the confidence they had had in the new weapon up to this attack.

Connolly had been hearing reports about his own county which had made him anxious. The Longford Column had been protecting Ballinalee almost as a standing garrison. At night there was an inspection to see that all people had left the town so that its defenders would not have the added task of protecting the population. Tired of waiting for an enemy who knew that a reprisal would not now be too easy, the column lay out beside the road between Edgeworthstown and Granard at Ardagullion Bog. They had buried two mines in the road and they had waited patiently in the snow and in damp trenches for close on three days. On the evening of 1 December, they saw a glare of a Very light in the cold air from the Ballinalee direction, and they knew the Tans had come back. They had returned guided by good Orange information. They had burned a few houses and taken over a large shop with a grocery and a bar. They had given the owner, Paddy Farrell, 25 minutes to clear himself and his family out of their way.

Quickly plans were made for an attack, and two days later on Sunday 3 December 1920 it came. The roads surrounding Ballinalee were patrolled and held by IRA. Recently they had looked upon the town as their own, but the proposed ambush had drawn them away from it. A few Tans were in front of their new post within shot distance of a section which was waiting behind a wall opposite them. Eugene Kilbride, the Longford Brigade Engineer, tested the exploder and ran his hands over the connections, then when he was satisfied Seán Duffy carried the heavy mine in his arms and laid it down on the window sill on the gable end. Then he walked quietly back to Kilbride who pressed the plunger sharply down. There was a heavy boom as the mine exploded. It had not damaged the wall sufficiently but it had blown a hole in it. Straw and petrol were alternately thrown in by the attackers, but the floor inside was of stone, and as there was no wood for the fire to grip the defenders were able to quickly quench the flames. The column men worked under the cover of rifle fire, but they had to give up the attempt.

A Tan inside made use of Farrell's piano. He played 'God Save the King' and the solemn chords were interrupted by the sharp cracks of the Lee-Enfields, the glaring path of tracer bullets and the stuttering rat-tat-tat of the defenders' machine guns. The attack was called off by Seán MacEoin as there was no method now of putting the house on fire. As the column retired, they were fired on by local Orangemen as they went beyond the town. Some of them had come out into the open, had travelled around with Tans and had pointed out houses to them. Some of them were later executed for the assistance they had given to the RIC and the Tans. Next day Farrell's, which was an isolated building, was judged too dangerous to hold in its shattered condition. A few houses were taken over including the village school. That day Seán Connolly's house was burned and although the column tried to protect Seán Duffy's and Seán MacEoin's houses, they were also burned.

Ever since the attempted destruction of Ballinalee on 3 December, the village people became accustomed to leave it at night. Always their bundles were ready so that they could leave suddenly and their small treasures had been spread around in houses outside. The Connollys had long been expecting that their house would be destroyed by reprisal parties as soon as they came again to Ballinalee, but a month had passed. The family had again been warned by the Column men on 12 December to be on their guard. Old John Connolly, his wife, Margaret, and some of the children, had been sleeping at night with friends for close on five weeks. In the daytime they would return to their house with ears on the alert for lorry noises or shots which might announce a hostile approach. Maura Connolly, one of the children, had been out that Monday to visit her home for she had been staying with relatives. There was no one in the house and the neighbours had left the neighbouring houses as well. She had remained for some time to look after fowl and to look at cattle, but as she went away she heard the noise of rifle shots which continued their echoes. Four lorries of Tans had swirled by the house. On their way they had opened fire on the neighbourhood first to reduce it to the King's Peace – as if it had given birth to the attack. They placed a charge at a gable end, and they blew it up. Then they attacked the house as if that too had been responsible for the onslaught on their post. An explosive charge was placed at one gable and when the smoke and dust of the sudden uplift was over, the gable disappeared. They sprayed petrol on the inside of the walls and on the furniture, then with a roar the spreading gas put the house into a sudden bonfire. The unresisting outhouses went down one by one with appropriate yells. Reeks of turf, of hay and straw spread their separate blazes into the winter sky. The Tans had ample petrol and time for an all out attack. The beasts outside in the outhouses had already been shot but a few remained in nearby fields which helped to empty a few magazines. Finally, frightened hens and geese, more staunch in their resistance, made something of a target for men of war. The only living things which escaped were a few calves a few fields away which they had not noticed. Connolly, according to his sister, Maura, did not know what had happened to his house, until one day when eating his lunch in the open, he happened to read a paragraph on the paper which had been wrapped around the well buttered farl of cakebread.

Chapter 8

Dublin Castle, December 1920

———————

After Christmas 1920, Seán Connolly went to Dublin to report to GHQ. He was anxious to get back to Longford if he was permitted to return, but he had work to do in Roscommon first. There should be some changes in the North Roscommon Brigade staff, he felt. The brigadier, Seamus Ryan, would need to be replaced by a man more in accord with activity. Connolly had planned his own operations in the area, but it was time to have a staff in unison with whatever fight the brigade could work up to. The Chief-of-Staff, Cathal Brugha, had suggested an election for brigadier, leaving the senior officer as vice-brigadier, and that, it was felt, would solve the problem for the time being.

I had myself organised both North and South Roscommon Brigades in 1918, but it was then too early in the lack of activities which were the test of men for me to judge certain officers. Connolly had stayed in houses I had not been in and perhaps the fact of a stranger moving up and down through the battalions had made it safe for another man to do his work without undue talk of his presence. The most dangerous area for me had been around Carrick-on-Shannon. I had had many narrow escapes from police and soldiers who knew I was close to them and who had a desire to be close to me. A few times I had to cross the Shannon into Leitrim and Longford. Connolly had slept in the shed beside the home of Jim Feely of Boyle whose family had been masons for long generations. I had been using a chisel and mallet at intervals on a piece of limestone, but I had found it difficult to keep the edges of my lettering from chipping at random. The workshed was on the side of the road a few hundred yards south of the town, and as I worked on my slab one day, I heard a curious passer-by talk to Jim Feely.

'Who's the new lad who's working for you there?'

'Oh. he's a new apprentice, and he's just beginning to serve his time.'

'Well he's new alright', was the judgement, 'for he's making no great shapes at the letters.'

While Connolly was in Dublin, he met Pat Mullooly who was then working on the railway in Dublin. He was to be sent down to the Brigade to help. I had first met Mullooly in July of 1918 in Kilglass on the ridge which overlooks the Shannon feeding lakes beneath it. I had planned to disarm the guard of 22 soldiers who then held Carrick railway station. Mullooly armed with a .22 rifle was with me on the night of the raid as we waited on a road close to the station for our men to meet us, but at seven o'clock only seven of the 22 picked had reached us. Mullooly and Mick Dockery were to be dressed in RIC uniforms which had been borrowed from a dramatic class which was to have played 'The Rising of the Moon'. I was to hold up the night goods train some distance away, remain beside the engine driver and have the engine halted in such a place that a certain wagon which contained men from Carrick area would be then convenient for their help. The two RIC men were by this time to have been talking to the sentries whom they were to hold up when I rushed the guard room, followed by the wagon men who would grab arms and ammunition. The plan, however, remained a plan. A Volunteer officer had told the men who had been mobilised that the military were lying in wait around the station and that no Volunteer could now go near it.

In December of 1920, I was sitting on a few yellowish hard rectangles which were known as army biscuits, in the Auxiliary guardroom in Dublin Castle.[1] One of the guards was examining his Lewis gun which faced down the cul de sac of Exchange Court. As I watched him two prisoners were brought in just before curfew. I knew one of them, as I looked at the spare figure and the thin sardonic face of Mullooly. He did not recognise me, and I was pleased. My hair was rough and long, and I had at least four days' beard. My clothes were torn and my shirt could have done with a good lather, but I could not get a change of clothes as I was trying to look like a small farmer, though by this time I was more like a tramp.

Next day I was sweeping the floor near to the prisoners' benches and biscuits when I came close to Mullooly who was reading a paper. 'Do you remember the settle bed in Kilglass and the long, long night?' I asked. He looked at me hard for a while as if he was trying to telescope two visions, but my battered face, and my angled nose would have been the envy of any belligerent tinker who had survived his rivals at the horse fair in Ballinasloe. Then as I saw by the surprise in his eyes and his 'Holy God' that he knew me, I said quickly 'My name is Stewart, I'll see you in the washroom.' The reference to the settle bed which he understood, meant the night when Michael, his brother, and I had spent in a small settle bed near Kilglass. There might have been room for two of us, but the third was a strain on the bed's hospitality. Mullooly, who had been asleep awoke suddenly, and gripped me.

'What's wrong with you?' he asked, 'did you hear a noise or what?'

'Do you think Pat', I asked him, 'will the long, long night ever end?'

When we met in the washhouse, he asked:

'Do you think they know anything about you?'

'Not yet', I said.

'Well, thank God for that, but judging by your face they don't like you overmuch. I noticed this morning that they called all of us in the morning, but when they came to you, they kicked you and cursed you about Macroom.'

Each successive guard of five had been told that I had been in the Macroom ambush, as they called Kilmichael, where 17 Auxiliaries had been killed. 'They had been chopped with hatchets', their own report had said, and so I was a curiosity to them and a test of their individual bitterness or detachment. I was one of the few prisoners who admitted that I belonged to the IRA, and having admitted my attachment I had to create my own standard of how I should act then in the hands of the British. I was a stalking horse for their doubts or for their attempts to resolve their propaganda when faced with a protagonist who attempted to show no sign of the strain that ate like a Spartan fox at his guts. Some of them talked to me in a friendly manner which I at once accepted, others turned a bitter look of hatred on me, or I would catch a concentrated stare of venomous intensity focused like a searchlight to make their lack of understanding clear to them.

'Any chance of you getting out of here?'

'I don't think so', I replied. 'I've been watching ever since I came in here. I'll have to fight it out I think by grabbing one of their guns or a rifle when they are off their guard.'

'And what would you do then?' he asked curiously.

'Then I might get out the main gate, or if I was concerned, I'd try to get the Intelligence Room and there have a more equal argument with Major King and Captain Hardy.'[2]

He shook his head, 'I don't see any hope for you, lad.'

Mullooly and his friend, Mick O'Connell,[3] had had trouble with some soldiers in a bar near the Castle gate. They had knocked down a few of the men in khaki but a foot patrol had cut them off in Dame Street. I had heard them both protesting their loyalty in the guardroom and I had admired Mullooly's aggressive obstinacy. That night I noticed, whenever I woke up to covertly watch the guard, their movements and the passing in and out of secret service men whom they talked about when these footsteps faded into silence, that Mullooly was also awake.

We carried on many a strange conversation in the guardroom as cabalistic as any magic ritual being made up of place names, personal names, nicknames and the hidden life and history of North Roscommon as I had seen and gathered into my web. An enigmatic remark would be instantly interpreted, or it would take some time to work out and so a kind of local 'Finnegans Wake' was formed before us. Double and treble allusions, hair trigger jokes at which we would find it hard to keep straight faces yet we would not pretend to a shared intimacy. Mullooly, who had a quick intelligence, made his own astringent and cryptic remarks, which normally flowed from him in conversation, now twisted their tortuous course for my misleading. His greatest difficulty was in checking his spate of talk. Our conversations were laconic at times and all attempts to dissuade our faces from a contagious laugh were hard on the rib ends. Once, I burst in a quick explosion and in a sudden silence the entire guard looked at me in gloomy concern and distrust.

Mullooly kept his eyes, as I had been keeping mine, on every movement inside the guardroom and his ear to the prisoners as well as to the guards, for I had warned him about the possibility of touts being thrown in for a few days with the curfew prisoners. I had grown a seeming film of indifference to my gaze as I noted everything which might be of use and I judged each member of the guard in turn. Usually their habits of discipline were somewhat relaxed just before dawn and also a while before their term of duty was finished.

Before Mullooly had been thrust into us I had been wandering in my mind among early Italian paintings. I was endeavouring to recall when certain frescoes and temperas of particular painters were at that time, recalling as well as I could the compositions, and trying also to build up their colour schemes. I had always carried a few coloured reproductions around with me on my wanderings and at the most incongruous moments I had studied a painter. Now in this guardroom as swarthy with menace as any Italian city had been for its earlier painters to work in, I had no check on the correctness of my concentration. I was working hardest on Piero della Francesca, Masaccio, Lorenzo Monaco and Sandro Botticelli, remembering pages from the good library of Count George Plunkett or arguments with Seoirse and Eoin Plunkett. Soon I would be cormorant deep in an argument with myself about colour or form, and from a satisfying memory of delight I would surface again as a prisoner of the Auxiliaries.

Mullooly and O'Connell were quickly released, mainly because O'Connell had once been a driver to a Northerner, who had been killed in France. One of the Auxiliaries, now sergeant of the guard, had been a great friend of that officer in France. The two prisoners were given a paper to sign after they had protested many times their feelings of loyalty to the Crown and its forces. The paper, full of whereas and whenas, was first read aloud to them. They were to report to the nearest police barracks whenever the police judged that their presence was necessary. That evening as I walked up and down the narrow passage where Dick McKee, Peadar Clancy and Conor Clune had been bayoneted and shot the previous month, I saw Mullooly walk up to the gate which led towards the guardroom of 'F' Company. He handed a parcel to the sergeant of the guard who watched our movements in the open, and as he passed out the gate he waved his hand to me in farewell. The Auxiliary came over to me. 'That fellow', he said, as he examined the contents, 'asked me to give these to the red-headed tinker for he certainly needs them, so here they are.' He handed me a shirt and a pair of trousers. 'I don't know what a tinker means', he added, but I did not respond.

That night Mullooly met Michael Collins and and Gearoid O'Sullivan in a house in Church Street. Seán Connolly was present. Collins had questioned Mullooly about Dublin Castle, and he had mentioned the details I had told him about the garrison Auxiliary company, their routine and guard system and other information I had overheard from my changing guards or had seen in the various places I had been through inside the Castle bounds. Later in the week they met again. Mullooly had been meeting a man who had worked in the canteen in the Castle, but he seemed unwilling to take risks, and there was now no way by which contact could be made with me. Collins knew I had no chance of survival if it was found out who I was, and I did not expect any extension on my possibility of living, even under my assumed name. Connolly talked about the changes which would be made in the brigade staff of North Roscommon and the chance of carrying out a few barrack attacks. Mullooly was soon to return to his area to help them. Connolly who came down by train to Virginia Road was met at Finea by Bill Doherty, Seán MacEoin and Frank Davis. He moved around among his friends at different houses, for a wanted man had always a number of houses where he was as much a member of the family as the boys and girls of that household, and as affectionately regarded by them all. This was a real holiday for him. He saw his own people and quieted their fears as much as he could. Talk and song made him think of his fiddle, but his own fiddle had been on the fire wall of his house as was customary, and it had added its small blaze of the memory of song and dance and the unity of tradition to the conflagration made by the Tans.

As was customary when four or five comrades got together, there was soon an interchange of information about what had happened in their respective volunteer spheres of control. That meant a summary of events in the area in which each of the officers worked and a frank dealing with people who did or did not do their duty in relation to events. Longford, Leitrim and Roscommon ran the gauntlet of talk and criticism. The intimate details of the personnel of IRA, RIC, Tans and military were carefully sieved, the possibility of attacks on posts and on patrols was gone into in minute detail, and as carefully propounded as operations. Remembered ground and a tradition of land use were now to be employed against intruders, whether they belonged to our own like the RIC or stopgaps as were the Tans and Auxiliaries, or the hereditary active enemy, the British military. They, the military, had in times past created their own forces of alien tradition and disloyalty and as long as they held power or spread their seed, they added additional contributions to the Irish maze. The cold had restricted enemy movement on snow-covered roads where melting ice again froze rapidly. The Longford Column had been disbanded for the Christmas season and both forces had to temporarily cease active hostility.

Chapter 9

Roscommon, October 1920–February 1921
Peace Efforts, Strokestown, Elphin

Near Tulsk, Bill Doherty and Seán Connolly met Dan O'Rourke who was in charge of South Roscommon. Connolly was anxious to get some little activity out of the border area, for that would relieve pressure on the North Roscommon Brigade when the attacks he had planned in his mind became actual. At the end of his demands for cooperation, Connolly mentioned that from his talks with people in Dublin he felt they would not get a Republic, and that sudden shock upset the three of them. The two officers did not talk much on the road back to Ballinameen, but before Connolly reached Jack Roche's, he told Doherty that Michael Collins had instructed him before he left Dublin to get as many reliable men as he could from the IRA into the Irish Republican Brotherhood, for continued resistance. That organisation had not been given much thought by Connolly as he had been too busy for the past year in making full use of the Volunteers to render occupation by the British costly and undesirable. That conception of the IRB as the rearguard of staunchness was being less and less considered in the country as resistance developed.

There had been peace stirs ruffling against the winds of war since October, but there had been no urgency about them. In November Dr Patrick Joseph Clune, Archbishop of Perth, who was a chaplain to the Australian Catholic forces, had been visited by influential Englishmen, who suggested that he meet David Lloyd George. On 1 December, the British premier asked the Archbishop to visit Arthur Griffith. The previous day, Arthur Henderson and another English Labour Party leader had been to Mountjoy Jail to see Arthur Griffith, who was then the acting head of the Republican government. The two English members of Parliament were anxious to help any talks which might prepare the way for a truce. Henderson was Chairman of the Labour Party Commission of Inquiry, which had come to Ireland on 30 November. Previously, the English Labour Party in October had proposed in the House of Commons:

> That this house regrets the present state of lawlessness in Ireland and the lack of discipline in the armed forces of the Crown and is of opinion that an independent investigation should at once be instituted into the causes, nature and extent of reprisals on the part of those whose duty is the maintenance of law and order.

But the request had been refused. The Labour Party had then set up its own commission.

Dr Clune met Griffith in Mountjoy Jail for a long talk; then later he saw Diarmuid O'Hegarty and Collins. On the outside O'Hegarty was attached to General Headquarters Staff, but he was also Secretary to Án Dáil. When Griffith, who was Acting President, had been brought as a prisoner to Mountjoy, he was met in 'C' Wing by a reception committee. He was a prisoner now, he said, and he would act under the orders of his wing commander. Leo Henderson was in charge of 'C' Wing. Before Griffith and Eoin MacNeill went out to meet Dr Clune, Griffith informed the wing commander and asked his permission to meet the Archbishop. When Griffith returned later that evening and reported to Leo Henderson, he was very pleased about his interview with Dr Clune.

'The British, I think, mean business this time', he said. 'I want you to consider the military aspect of the situation for that has not yet been discussed.'

A truce was being considered, which envisaged a cessation of hostilities for a conference, but the Dublin Castle authorities wanted a surrender of arms first, although Lloyd George did not require that surrender.

Dr Clune would have a very different impression of the men he had met in jail and those whom he had seen on the outside who were being continually raided for, than would their opponents whom he had already talked to in London. While he was in Dublin he heard about the manner in which his nephew had been killed in Dublin Castle with Dick McKee and Peadar Clancy. Conor Clune[1] had not belonged to the IRA nor was there any reason for his arrest save that he had been in Vaughan's Hotel when a party of Auxiliaries had raided it on the evening of 20 November. They had evidently come to catch some of the Headquarters Staff who had been at a meeting in a room upstairs. There was continuous contact between Griffith and Collins through a few friendly warders who would bring concealed letters to Kirwin's public house in Parnell Street and then carry back replies from Collins. In this way a small group inside could be immediately aware of what was happening in Án Dáil circles in Dublin.

When Dr Clune returned to London on 8 December, he found that three holes, from the British viewpoint, had been torn in the stiffness of Irish resistance. The tears, like an Irish Triad, had been interpreted as signs of national weakness when they could have come from personal weakness, disrespect to their sworn allegiance or from mistaken sense of authority. Roger Sweetman had written a letter to the papers. Galway County Council had passed a resolution and Father Michael O'Flanagan had taken it on himself to attempt to establish a direct contact with Lloyd George.

Galway County Council had given its allegiance to Dáil Éireann. The Council consisted of 32 members, eight of whom formed a quorum, but six members only attended the meeting. Not satisfied with expressing their views at the meeting, their resolutions were published in the daily papers:

> We therefore as adherents of Dáil Éireann request that body to appoint three delegates to negotiate a truce. We further request that the British will appoint three delegates who will have power to arrange a truce and preliminary terms of peace honourable to both countries. We consider that the initiative lies with the British Government who should withdraw the ban on the meetings of Dáil Éireann.

The six members then passed a resolution: 'viewing with sorrow the shootings, burnings, reprisals and counter-reprisals now taking place all over Ireland', and it further declared that any side refusing to accept these proposals should be held by the world responsible for any further shootings or burnings that might take place. Copies of the resolution were ordered to be sent to each county council, Dáil Éireann, Lloyd George, the Irish bishops, Catholic and Protestant, and to the British Labour delegation. Professor Breathnach, TD, who presided over the Council, said that the Sinn Féin movement was a constructive and not a destructive one.

Father O'Flanagan, who was Vice-President of Sinn Féin, had gone to London with Sir James O'Connor to meet the outskirts of authority. When he came back to Ireland, he sent a telegram to Lloyd George. However well meaning the undisciplined and ill-timed intentions of the Triad were, the publicity of their intervention gave the British the impression that there was dissension on the Republican front. To the British, Sinn Féin represented the entire resistance movement, though technically it was a political organisation which did not take part in armed opposition but did help to implement any decrees from Dáil Éireann. Since Án Dáil had been proscribed as being illegal, the British would not accept that it had any authority or that it represented the people who had elected it. Lloyd George made use of the weak spots to demand a surrender of arms in the Commons on 10 December. By this time Dublin Castle had assured the British Cabinet that the Republican movement was weakening. The rebels were being hard pressed, they reported; consequently this was a sign of a break up of their strength and support. A truce was what their now demoralised forces needed in which to rest and gather strength.

Lloyd George had his own difficulties. There was his opportunist mind and his flea hopping propensity to adjust to Liberal Party opposition in England, and national strength in Ireland. Tory opposition in Army and Parliament was always hostile to any acknowledgement that government in Ireland was slowly becoming impossible. Dublin Castle had always hoped that another spell of armed authority would crack Irish solidity, but they were always in need of reinforcements for the Royal Irish Constabulary and the military. Sir Henry Wilson, General Sir Nevil Macready commanding the troops in Ireland and Major General Boyd of the General Command in Dublin District met in London. They were in favour of imposing martial law at once.

On 8 December, Dr Clune met Lloyd George to report his conversations with people whom he had met with in Ireland. On the same day the Cabinet had agreed to use martial law in four counties, Cork, Kerry, Limerick and Tipperary, but they would first permit an interval before the proclaiming to allow priests for two Sundays to appeal at Masses for arms to be first surrendered to them. This extension was not permitted, and on 10 December martial law was proclaimed in the four counties. Next day, on 11 December, 'K' Company of Auxiliaries, acting under the order of its officers, had burned a large part of Cork city. Auxiliaries were demonstrating that they were a law unto themselves, for under martial law reprisals instead of being haphazard and unacknowledged, would now have to be carried out under the orders of Major General Sir Peter Strickland who was in command of the Sixth Division. This indiscipline strengthened Lloyd George's hand against extreme Tories and militarists.

Dr Clune, on his return to Dublin, visited MacNeill and Griffith. He told them the effect the Triad had had on the proposed Truce. The Most Rev. Dr Michael Fogarty, Bishop of Killaloe, accompanied him on his entry to Mountjoy. Eamonn Duggan and Michael Staines, who were also prisoners, could listen to the morning's discussions each evening. The jail talks continued. A month's truce was again around its many echeloned corners. The British premier had been able to make full use of the burning of Cork and the surrender of arms was no longer demanded. The Auxiliary company concerned was ordered to leave Cork. It left in a truculent mood, the cadets wearing as an extra cap badge a small round of burnt cork as a symbol of their latest military heat. Arthur Griffith was now convinced that the Truce would take place some time after Christmas. When Leo Henderson had asked him earlier in the negotiations what would then happen, Griffith said that discussions would begin and in about six months' time the terms of a treaty would be ready for agreement. The Castle, however, backed by Sir Hamar Greenwood, and the military supported by Sir Henry Wilson, pressed for the surrender of arms. Father O'Flanagan had gone to London, against the advice of Eamon de Valera, who had returned from the United States, and Collins. He had been repudiated by Peadar O'Keefe, the Acting Secretary of Sinn Féin, who pointed out that he had not received authority to act by the Standing Committee of that organisation.

Seán Connolly had heard of the negotiations when in Dublin, and Collins had cursed freely at the individuals who were misusing their judgement but that is an extremely ladylike interpretation of his storm-tossed words. Connolly was now increasingly eager to show that there was no weakness in North Roscommon, the first constituency to return a candidate who would not go to the House of Commons, and the parliamentary area where Father O'Flanagan had held a gap and had defied his own bishop.

In January 1921, at a North Roscommon Brigade Council in Hillstreet, Mick Dockery who had been vice brigadier was elected brigadier, the brigadier, Seamus Ryan, was made his assistant, Jack Clancy of Drumlion became adjutant and Pat Mullooly, quarter-master. It was planned to make simultaneous attacks on patrols in the area on 5 January. In Strokestown men lay out on the hill which rose up from the entrance gate to Park House which was yet a military post. They used their rifles on the sentry post to keep the Lancers wondering if an attack was being made on them, while up the street a policeman was wounded. He died on the following day. There were two police wounded in Tarmonbarry and one in Elphin. Connolly with a few men from Mantua and Ballinameen held the approaches to Frenchpark Barracks. The rain poured down steadily on the waiting men. One group halted all whom they met with and placed a guard on them so that no word could reach the RIC. Often enough, false information of police movements would be sent to a battalion by a local company or people, who were afraid of reprisals on their village, and would pass on word to the RIC that strangers were in the neighbourhood. Three men with shotguns, under John Kelly from Ballinameen, waited in a lane, 25 yards from the door of Ballinameen Barracks, and as they peered through the driving rain they heard footsteps come down a path. Steps approached the barracks, and when they were getting ready to fire the door opened and the silhouette of a girl's head was shaped against the faint light from the inside. Kelly hastily shoved down the other two shotguns with a rapid arm push.

Next day near Ballinameen John Kelly was busy making buck-shot pellets with which he proposed to refill the empty cartridge cases strewn on the kitchen table. While he worked at the molten lead, a young lad, Joe Moran, saw a strong force of military and police, who had come from Boyle, making their way across the fields. He knew he would find Connolly in Jack Roche's some distance away, and he thought he might be in time to give him warning. He ran quickly across the bare fields, but a running man of any age was then always a tempting target for military and police rifles. Crouching behind denuded banks, Moran made for Roche's, but Connolly and a few men who were inside heard the rifle volleys and had gone out through the back fields. In the meantime Kelly's father had come back a little while before this to warn his son that he had seen police in the near distance as he was giving an armful of hay to calves. John Kelly quickly bundled up buckshot and cartridges. He carried out a pile of weapons which he had gathered up from hiding places, and which had a coat of rust on them. He stuck them in the brow of a bank, then dragging his legs slowly, with his head bent, he passed across the line of advancing police who did not bother about the old man who moved within shooting distance of them.

The general activity of the previous night of 5 January had brought out Auxiliaries, Tans and military in punitive strength. In some houses they split up wooden floors with crowbars and bayoneted mattresses until feathers flurried through the house like heavy snow flakes. They smashed the glass on oleographs of Robert Emmet which they then placed under their muddy boots. They had not been sure about Emmet at one time. They had often mistaken him for the victor of Waterloo, but his green uniform often betrayed him even if there was not a Peeler present who could identify the rebel. Photos of 1916 leaders were torn up or thrown into the kitchen fire. Flour bags and oats for the hens, which had their cosy corner near the hob, were holed with bayonets and the contents thrown out into the miry yard. A Tan or Auxiliary with that commanding gesture, the quick lunge of a butt end, would sweep a dresser clear of its carefully treasured cups, jugs and plates, which would only come into use in their entirety for a wake or at the breakfast which followed the local 'station'.

They burned a number of houses, and in others they threw furniture out in the yard where they chopped it to inconsiderate fragments. They wounded a few bullocks as they grazed on the winter fields, and they swung up their rifles at their customary targets, geese, which they brought back as evidence of their marksmanship to the barracks pot. They could readily plead extenuating circumstances for some of the geese were shot trying to escape and that was a reason in use by military and RIC to justify their use of ammunition. Dogs did not like men in uniform. Some of them made determined efforts to protect the houses in which they had been brought up, but if they showed any spirit they were quickly served with a bullet. The whole family would mourn the unnecessary killing of the dog. This smashing of the dresser delph was bitterly felt by the women of the house. In a countryside where people had few possessions these shining coloured ranks of plates, mugs and jugs brightened up austerity.

The Crown forces were searching for individual men whose names the RIC had passed on. Their failure to find the wanted men was atoned by their zeal in destruction. They captured a lieutenant of the Elphin Company. He was repeatedly beaten with rifle butts and fists until they reached a river. They threw him into it from the bridge as they were on their road to Carrick, and when he reached the town his clothes were stiffened with ice.

Early in February Connolly was ready to attack Elphin Barracks. He had asked help from Carrowroe on the eastern slopes of Slieve Bawn and from men in South Roscommon. Pat Madden, from the

South with a few rifles and five men, met the Carrowroe Volunteers some ten miles from Elphin. They moved on through the darkness until met by scouts, then they were guided to a deserted house in which they bedded down on straw. The old man who lived next door supplied them with food, but he was afraid to look at any of them for fear he might afterwards be questioned by the British in too robust a manner. In the house where they waited that day there were mines which they were expected to carry in towards Elphin in the evening.

A cart with a broken shaft and an indifferent ass ornamented with oddments of rope for harness left Bessy Kelly's with a load of mines, cart boxes and gas bombs the next evening. The broken shaft and the improvised harness were to spare better fittings in case the ass and cart might be captured. The ass had a good escort of Ballinameen men, for Connolly always used this company when he had any work nearby. They went south of the town then across country to join the Carrowroe and South Roscommon men. The plan was for them to move in to Elphin between eight and nine o'clock, before the pubs would close, so that the movement of groups would cause no question. A section would then take over a house to the east of the barracks. Towns closed down for the night early that winter, leaving the streets to the RIC and Tans to patrol who challenged anyone they met with. Their interpreter of safety would be a policeman who had been long stationed in the town, and he would be able to identify any men from the district or be wary as soon as he knew they were strangers.

The South Roscommon men waited for their guides who were to take them across country to Tubbercurry, the holy well, which was their meeting place for destruction. The boys who came from Killina Company to lead them said they did not know their way across the bogs, but the eleven strangers seemed to doubt them and their lack of knowledge. They had to go around by the roads, which were more risky in case of an accidental meeting with enemy for these men unaware of their surroundings. The roundabout road journey took up more of their time, and it was time that concerned them most. Martin Fallon, who was tall and able, carried a cement mine in a sack. He regretted his strength after a short time on that frosty night. The mine was awkward to carry for it seemed composed of sharp edges of concrete which embedded themselves in his shoulders, and its angularity added to the grievous burden of its weight which was about 60 pounds.

When they reached Tubbercurry the time was out of joint, and the atmosphere was anything but religious. The fluent curses of the Southern men voiced the protest of their unnecessarily long journey, but the irritation at their lateness provoked a stronger crispness of adjectives which were fit to dry up the blessings that the water near them might have given to the undertaking. It was half nine, and it was now too late to venture into the town. Seán Connolly was furious at the delay and the men from the Elphin Battalion would have been content enough to blame the men from other battalions. Connolly knew, as did anyone who had screwed practically untried men up to an attack, how important it was to carry out the plan at the appointed time and on the arranged-for night. Here they were now with mines, cart boxes, fuse and rifles, yet the failure could not be blamed on the strangers. The heavy mines were placed on projecting stones under a bridge from where they could be removed the following day. He ordered the men to return home, and he hid his own frustration but disappointed groups wandered off in the frosted darkness. The Carrowroe and South Roscommon men had among them John Gibbons and Patrick Buzzer Farrell, ex-soldiers who had not been impressed by their traipsing along roads to find they were late and would now have to return to their own townlands. They wanted to lie on the watercourse up the street and wait for a patrol but that too had to be gainsayed [*sic*]. With them at the time was Seán Bergin who was soon to meet with a summary death at the hands of the military and to give rise to a ballad.

> Seán Bergin said that he was proud to die for Ireland's cause
> He did the deeds that should be done by all our Irish boys
> Saying goodbye to Tipp'rary and to every vale and glen
> And to my faithful comrade boys in the woodlands of Loughglynn

It was in no such lyrical mood that the men of South Roscommon said goodbye to the country around Elphin as they shaped for home, some fourteen miles away. They heard music in the frosty air as they were strung out in protection as a patrol but they soon found it was a busy crosscut making the few trees there were fewer. The outpost had not been told that the operation had been cancelled.

This was the second attempt on the Elphin garrison, and so far they had the luck on their side. 'I wonder', Seán Connolly said to a Strokestown man, 'if it could be the parish priest praying for the safety of the town'. As soon as the post was attacked, it was expected there would be a reprisal party at work unless the assault was a complete success. That often gave a local garrison so much to think about that it was not anxious to endure any unnecessary risk once the surrounding area had proved its competence. An attack postponed had its dangers, that he knew. It would run as a theme in men's minds until the real attack took place, and there was always the danger of being over secretive and the risk of certain men, who might allow it to appear that they knew more than other people by a boasting, or by letting slip a remark when they were off their guard. As well, an attack which had failed to come off might give a talk licence to men. They might think the project would never again be attempted and the thin web of surprise would be broken.

Connolly, however, thought that he could take Elphin. It was important now, he realised, to divert or lessen the pressure on

Longford which was being well raked by troops, and which was bearing more than its share of the load in holding the Midlands burden. There was a thatched house on either side of the barracks, and although a mixture of explosives and fire seemed to be the solution, or fire by itself, yet he did not care to risk the destruction of the house next door and perhaps a portion of the town as well as the barracks in the conflagration. Boyle and Doon Companies had seized two wagon loads of petrol which were to have gone on to Boyle Military Barracks, and these were now stored in a safe place in Boyle hospital by the Matron and the Master, who were both friendly. This supply could always be drawn on by the Volunteers.

Before the next attack Connolly sent Jim Feely of Boyle and Celia Roche, whose husband, Jack, had helped to prepare the improvised cart boxes, into Longford to borrow rifles. Mick Murphy, the Commandant of the 2nd Longford Battalion, had no rifles to lend. When the motor car reached Ballinalee district, it was found that the rifles were needed for a project of their own. At Dromod on the way back the car was held up by a strong patrol of Tans, who were convinced by Mrs Roche's tears and general distress that she was returning from a very sad funeral. The distress was somewhat strengthened by the dangerous burden of the dispatches she was carrying back to Seán Connolly. Rifles came on from Connolly's country before the Elphin plan was carried out.

The attack was due for the night of 11 February, but this time the local battalion alone was concerned in it. Elphin was a loyal town, unlike the people in Boyle or in Strokestown who were amplified ears for anything that might happen to their military or police. Volunteers could move in and out in safety to the town. Now, they had to converge from many sides. Riflemen covered the barracks from Mrs Kelly's, about 50 yards away on the eastern or Carrick side. Another section which had a view of the barracks was an equal distance to the west in Carney's lane. Seán Connolly with his section had under rifle cover quietly entered the house next door to the barracks. They removed a few lodgers and an invalid woman; and as they were taking out another woman, she tried to throw a jam pot out the back window. Maybe this was a prearranged signal as a warning to the RIC that the house was now hostile. Her mouth had to be covered with a large hand while she was being brought to safety for fear she might shout a warning. The police had not been aware of this removal of five or six people.

The day room was next door to the room in which Connolly was preparing his cement mine. Already a Volunteer who had visited the house had found that the room contained a fireplace. This meant that the barracks wall would be weaker at the grate and flue. Before this attack Connolly had been questioned about the strength of gelignite he had intended to use. The charge was scanty enough for the work it had to do. Maybe he gave more credit to the destruction power of gelignite than it deserved. Even if the mine case had been tamped with sandbags it would have been more reassuring, but he would have needed twice the amount of explosives used to ensure reasonable hope of a wall collapse. Now, cart boxes and the gas producing mixture in small snuff tins were passed out on the floor ready for use. Connolly thought the explosion would bring the supporting wall and the barracks ceiling down on top of the police who were then expected to be in the day room for roll call. The mine was connected up with cables and was shoved into the fireplace, then the section got away to the third gateway up the street. When the explosion came with a satisfactory boom the section again rushed back, but instead of a gaping breach there was a small hole about two feet wide. Connolly threw in a few cart boxes. Their explosion blew out the glass from the barracks windows on to the street but there had been no police in the day room. The garrison threw out hand grenades, fired with their rifles at the windows across the street and sent up their signals for reinforcements into the night sky. The riflemen outside fired an odd shot, as ammunition was scarce.

Connolly used his gas bombs through the hole in the wall and out of the barracks windows a mixture of flame and smoke spurted up on to the street. The brimstone and cotton waste went on fire first, the blasting powder helped to scatter the burning mixture, and pepper added to the discomfort. A Tan opened the barracks door and threw out a hand grenade but the riflemen outside failed to register their bullets. The fumes swirled away as further tin boxes were added, but the biting smoke did not come back through the hole. Folklore says that Mick Dockery threw a heavy bomb which exploded outside the barracks door as the police were rushing downstairs to surrender and that they again rushed upstairs to a safe place. The attack had been a failure. A few doors down there was a supply of paraffin which could have been used, but Connolly was unwilling to handle it. He sent word to the riflemen to withdraw slowly when his section had left Lalors, and the outposts, who had been busy making roads impassable in depth around the town, were ordered to go home.

For some days men waited with Seán Connolly for reprisal parties which they thought would destroy houses near the town. The first night they were close to Ballyroddy School, which some of the officers thought was in too exposed a position for them to hold, but they had to wait on until the dawn reduced their protection. The road was blocked at the bridge near the school. Men lay in position to a flank and in the rear of any enemy who might come that way. When the British halted at the obstruction they were to be attacked from two sides. It was thought that Auxiliaries and police would burn the houses of Seán Owens, the Battalion Commandant, and Jack Murphy, both of which were a distance from the roadside. One day they saw Auxiliaries and RIC in the distance. There was a small river, a tributary of Lough Gara, in between them. Connolly's men had a fine sweep of fire from their raised bank. The British, who were less than 500 yards away, saw the men in position but they did not come any closer. All that day the raiding Crown forces were well behaved and even polite as compared with their previous excursion on 6 January. Perhaps the presence of rifles or the other weapons strange to the locality, from mines through cart boxes to throat-catching fumes, may have impressed them, but on the other hand the humour may not have been on them.

A few days later Seán Connolly passed up towards Drumsna on his way to Longford. The North Roscommon men were sorry to see him leave them. He had been a friend to them and he had been easy to work with. They understood his numerous failures, but about his intentions of fighting and of making the brigade contribute in the general resistance to British rule and its authority by fixed bayonets, they were as anxious to help as he had made them. They knew how to make mines of different patterns, and how to use them and if they continued to carry out his training against patrols, convoys or barracks under the direction of their brigade officers they could, though poorly armed, make their auxiliary weapons felt. The brigade staff had been remarkable for their inactivity up to the time of his arrival, but now they would be judged in terms of the initiative shown by another officer and by the response of the men to his influence.

The North Roscommon area had been awakened from its long sleep, and though his influence had been directed mostly in the Elphin Battalion, yet Strokestown had co-operated and the other two battalion units were about to stretch themselves. Pat Mullooly, as he shook hands with Connolly, felt that he would not ever see him again alive. Connolly had been warned against Leitrim by all who said goodbye to him. He had been somewhat nervous himself for it was a backward area, and the brigadier had not been interested in operations. However, each area, he knew, judged its county neighbours pretty harshly. County jealousy might be a relict of clan prejudice or of distrust engendered by continual British manipulation in weakening areas deliberately by alternate alliances, espionage and ruthlessness. He hoped to come back soon to have another tussle with Elphin Barracks and to combine this area and Longford for an attack on Lanesborough. They watched his slow smile as his dark eyes in the swarthy face glinted. Then as he waved his hat at a distance they saw his blue-black hair swirled by the wind.

Chapter 10

Leitrim, January–April 1921
Flying Column, Sheemore, Selton Hill

———————

Michael Murphy, Commandant of the Second Longford Battalion, was sent by Seán Connolly into Leitrim in 1920 to look out for stills beyond the county border. The RIC hunt for the mechanism of illicit whiskey making depended upon the desire of the local sergeant for the colourless 'water of life' and his capacity for holding his personal supply in equilibrium. There was, of course, a certain watch kept on suspicious curls of smoke in boglands and on mountainy glens, for if the sergeant did not sound certain faucets of his information in the territory which did not furnish his supply, the County Inspector might hear of it through his other devious ways. An odd keg of what was supposed to be captured poteen would be ceremoniously emptied down a drain near the barracks in the presence of the martinet District Inspector, but the thirsty sergeant would be only too aware that it contained water with little of the life. When the RIC withdrew from their isolated posts poteen makers became half underground. They could move about to sell their drink in far away places and they could work either in the daytime or at night as it suited them. With increased sales and increased security, the worm of greed worked its way into the ingredients in the still changing them for the worse, and when the wars gnawed the more, the number of times the liquid was distilled lessened. The RIC were now too busy protecting themselves or they were too absorbed in raiding for men and straining themselves for information to worry about illicit drink. The Republican police, who were now one of the special services in each IRA company, soon tapped the steady drip of information in their parish. They were able to hunt out all the secrets of their area, and they were helped by the neighbours. 'We'll have to make use of that Leitrim border sometime to fight in or to billet men in', said Seán Connolly, 'and now they're playing hell there with poteen'. Murphy found that even the younger lads were drinking themselves crooked. They were talking, which was a potential danger, about everything which came within their country ambit of information, save about where the stills were hidden. Murphy brought fifteen men with him four miles into Leitrim below the wooded edges of Lough Rinn. When they had destroyed six stills and mixed enough poteen with the bog water to set the wild geese drunk, they came back to Longford.

Connolly had also sent Frank Davis to move around through the Leitrim Brigade. He was to get an idea of the country and find out what was holding the men back there but he was told not to start anything in the way of a fight. Seamus Wrynn, the Brigade Vice-Commandant, Joe Beirne, Brigade Adjutant, John Joseph O'Reilly, Captain of Aughnasheelin Company, and Michael Baxter, he had already met during the attack on Arvagh Barracks. They were eager and helpful. Another county can be another world in Ireland and as difficult to access. Even though there is no visible boundary, yet the invisible barrier of time and of history can be abrupt as a mountain height. Davis had been introduced at a battalion council by Wrynn as 'Savage', and by this nom-de-guerre which covered his record he was known. It would prevent undue talk about his own name, which had been sent around to the adjoining RIC barracks. He went through the battalions, listening at council meetings, ferreting out men who would make fighting material and noting enemy strengths and their system of movement between posts.

Soon Davis found out how different from his home area a strange country could be. He had attended a Leitrim Brigade Council one night and when he was at his breakfast the next morning the girl of the house said to him:

'The soldiers were raiding all around early this morning.'

'But why didn't you call me when you heard the news?' he asked.

'Musha you're lucky', she replied, 'but they didn't come near the house, and I hid your big revolver where they would never find it.'

Davis left the table quickly, his face showing the incredulity that his mouth would have expressed in bad language. When he searched under his pillow he found his dependable companion was absent and he learned again his weapon discipline. The helpful girl had taken it from underneath his pillow as he lay asleep.

Davis was in Leitrim when Connolly came across the Shannon with a few Roscommon officers to meet the South Leitrim and Longford Brigade staffs at Reilly's of Drumlish in mid-February. There they exchanged information about enemy movements and methods, swapped details about individual officials and talked of the possibility of planning attacks in the areas not too heavily patrolled. There was an exchange of views on methods of harassing the British and of further co-operation between the units represented. These meetings kept the senior officers aware of what their neighbours were doing, made them sensitive to their difficulties and shortcomings. The Longford men had decided to lay an ambush for Tans who travelled in one or two lorries regularly between Granard and Longford. They would use road mines to destroy the two lorries. When the meeting had finished Davis told Connolly his impressions of South Leitrim, mentioning men who were sound, those who were inept, or who were trying to uphold activity. Connolly told him he would soon cross into Leitrim, and Davis was relieved for he wanted to get out of that county to link up with the Longford flying column.

Seán MacEoin had replaced Connolly as Longford Brigade Vice-Commandant. When the column had been started in November, there had been ample men to bring its strength up to 30. On that day, 1 November, the British had organised a general raid for officers and men throughout Ireland. GHQ had advised Longford of the British intention, and as a result no important officer was captured. There were now a big number of men who could no longer sleep in their homes and their services were practically entirely at the disposal of their battalions. That of course put an extra strain on the generosity of neighbours who fed them as if they belonged to their own households. MacEoin was in charge of the column, and he was also commandant of the 1st Longford Battalion and vice-commandant of the Longford Brigade. That triplication of ranks was unusual. The holding of a number of ranks by one man prevented the development of men who might have filled the vacancies. Connolly's few attempts against patrols in Roscommon had been very different from the assertion of the well-armed Longford men who had defended Ballinalee against an organised reprisal party of over seven lorries. Next, they had blown up portion of the gable of a house commandeered by Tans in Ballinalee and had harassed the new garrison.

The latest Longford exploit made Connolly envious. It took place on 2 February, the night before his first abortive attempt on Elphin Barracks. An ambush spoken of at the Drumlish meeting had been prepared at Clonfin near Ballinalee. Two lorries of Tans were expected, but instead came two tenders of Auxiliaries. A mine was blown underneath the first tender and after a sharp fight the Glenageary bonnets surrendered. They had lost six men killed and fourteen wounded. Each of them was armed with two Webley revolvers and a Lee-Enfield rifle, but when they were personally searched as an afterthought when they had surrendered their arms, a .32 revolver was found concealed on each Cadet. Evidently they had meant to use the hidden weapons when their captors were off their guard. That success meant a Lewis Gun, more than eighteen rifles and well over forty small arms.

Already some of the Leitrim men, Tom O'Reilly from Aughnasheelin company and another officer carrying side arms, weary because no attack was being planned in their brigade, visited MacEoin near Granard. They asked to be allowed to join up with his column, but previously there had been numerous applications from his own men to serve with him. MacEoin replied: 'The best man in this county will soon cross to your side and my advice is to get back and wait for him. He intends to get things moving as soon as he can, and I assure you that he'll make plenty of work for you.'

Before the last week of February 1921, Seán Connolly was in Owen Connor's house in Dernaheltamore, a good house, which meant that its generosity suffered as it was frequently used. Nearby was a column consisting mainly of officers from the battalion around Aughnasheelin. They had four good service rifles which had been captured the previous September when the East Yorks[1] had been removing bedding from the evacuated barracks of Carrigallen. Their lorry broke down in the bog at Corrawallen. Early next morning the guard of four soldiers was disarmed and the lorry was burned. They had now in addition three Mausers captured from Orangemen, and on each butt was stamped 'For God and Ulster'. The remainder of the column had good shotguns selected from the many which had been taken in house raids. They had received from GHQ before Connolly arrived, a collection of Belgian, Spanish and German automatics, which would have been suitable for shooting woodpigeons if one could get close enough to them. A quartermaster's work in an energetic area was difficult indeed. Every strange weapon meant a different source of ammunition supply outside of what could be captured within the county from the British.

Seán Mitchell, the South Leitrim brigadier, and Wrynn were with Connolly at Connor's. The column men were told how to use mines until their instructor felt that each one of them knew his new mechanism thoroughly. They were shown how to make the various mines which their instructor had already taught the Roscommon men to make. When the mines were finished, he lectured them on their application and showed them how they could be used. Each man then, he felt, was able to make a mine if necessary, and capable of using it in action with an electrical contact. Finally, he exploded a large road mine on a mountain, and the men were satisfied that the deep crater produced would have a stirring effect on an armoured Lancia or even on an armoured car.

The Leitrim men were content now. They could see the beginning of the work which MacEoin had spoken of to Tom O'Reilly. They were busy collecting broken pot-ovens, disused boilers in which potatoes had been boiled and pummelled for fowl, ass boxes and sand. They had seen mines laid down on roadways and they had studied the mechanism of improvised grenades. This was a good area in the best battalion of the brigade. It was backed by mountains which changed colour from swarthy drabness to the speedy light patches which overhead clouds threw into relief below. As always the hill people were friendly and as sound as spring water. The column had been inclined to keep to this stretch of country from which they could quickly move back to higher ground towards the slopes of Slieve Anierin. The Leitrim flying column was practically composed of officers, mainly for the reason that they were being looked for by the British, and capture at the time varied in result with the mood or the composition of the force which made men prisoners. The reason for the forming of a group of men under arms might have justified itself in the early autumn of 1920, but it was no longer a vindication. Columns had been organised not to protect individuals but to fight, to use their available arms on the British, and to defend the growing institutions of the Republic. 'The King's Peace' as a justification for a man holding the profession of arms had often been adduced as a reason for their use. In Ireland arms were borne to maintain the Peace of the Republic.

The narrow waist of country seven miles in width which ran across from Lough Allen to the mountainous Cavan border, cut off South Leitrim from the North Leitrim Brigade. The mountain core ran across from the suggestive Seltanna saggart through Slieve Anierin to Benbrack in Cavan, and through it three roads linked up with the north. Cavan was inactive and by its inactivity was a foreign country yet its western portion could have made as good fighting ground as there was to be had in this northerly area. The North Leitrim Brigade had impinged little on the British grip, and there was little touch with its fellow county. South of the mountains was a land of lakes connected by small streams interrupted by low lying isolated hills. Irregular quadrangles of road skirted the heights and roads were numerous. There were about three times as many roadways as there were in the North Roscommon area. Roads had not been torn up to restrict or prevent enemy movement and there was free access by them for their raiding purposes or for sudden round ups. The land was poor and rush infested. The soil was heavy, cold and wet, but there were creameries, a deal of chicken and turkey rearing, and pig fattening towards the border market town of Ballinamore. The farms were small and the land looked to be waterlogged. Forests had been steadily cut down by the Cootes who had been given large land grants when the Williamite Wars were at an end. There had been many ironworks on the slopes of Slieve Anierin and lower down at Drumshanbo and Ballinamore, and these had eaten up the timber which had once given shelter and protection to beasts, crops and men. There were now occasional trees only, and sallies or thorn bushes in the bordering banks.

There was a flat river valley from Drumshanbo, downwards to Roosky, on the east of the brigade, and a sudden extension above Carrick-on-Shannon led to the quiet beauty of wooded lakes towards Boyle. Below Carrick a great curve in the Shannon swung back above Drumsna and widened through a succession of lakes to Roosky. This river area changed slowly from the golden yellow sway of tall reeds in winter, which hid its wild water birds and confined the indigo reflections of harsh light, to the lush green edgings of late spring and summer against its blue and grey waters and the changing reflections of the clouds.

There were three battalions in the South Leitrim Brigade.[2] The RIC held Drumshanbo, Mohill, Carrick-on-Shannon and Ballinamore. The British used Carrick as their headquarters, but they had troops in Drumshanbo, Mohill and Ballinamore, where a party of Auxiliaries settled at intervals. There was a strong garrison in Lauderdale near to Ballinamore and in a house to the east of that town. There was another Auxiliary garrison, the Orangemen who were scattered but held strength if not the majority in numbers, from Ballinamore to Newtowngore and Carrigallen where they tilled the good land in the east of the county. Not so long since they had met regularly for drill and for weapon training, but now for their own safety, they had given up the military instruction. They had become an active intelligence force for the British at first, but the times had made them cautious, yet their Orange fringe had kept them hostile to liberalism, and indifferent to the nationalist effort, unlike a number of Unionists further South and West who had been changed by events.

Connolly made a big number of additional concrete mines which could be used against lorries and armoured Lancias. They weighed up to two hundred pounds, and he intended to put them in position on roads which were regularly patrolled by the British. He now selected suitable ambush positions, guided by local men who could tell him if friendly houses were close to the site. A trench was dug in the road, the mine which was sealed with pitch and felt was buried in its narrow grave, the road metal was carefully replaced and was stamped down. Positions had been also selected for mine operators to work from. These preparations would avoid the necessary preliminary digging just before an action and would avoid a disturbance of the road surface which might excite suspicion. Then, in the space of a week, the interfered-with road would look more like its normal self. That laying of mines gave him alternative positions to work from. Even if held by a few men they would be useful to delay reinforcements, or if used in conjunction with another position which had an armed party close to their mine, the British would run a double risk. They might think an additional column was in the neighbourhood and their movements by road would be slower and more careful.

Connolly decided to divide the column in two. He could take one half, the brigadier the other half, avoiding thus the risk of having too many untrained men together. There were now six additional rifles to divide. Pat Madden from South Roscommon had sent them on to Connolly on loan. Such a loan might seem either the right thing or the easy thing to do at the time, but anyone who served actively during the period can alone realise how gallant a gesture was the trusting of rifles to another area. There were battalions which would have raised a barrier of evasion, procras-tination and well thought out difficulties, in lending rifles to another battalion of their own brigade, unless their own men shouldered the weapons. As for the idea of lending rifles to another brigade, that was close on a miracle, only to take place when a very well trusted or admired man was responsible for an operation.

Connolly's mine was an additional strength to the divided column. It could replace rifles at the beginning of an action and by reducing the number of men it would make the force engaged less liable to information from their preliminary billeting or to observation. If, however, the mine failed to explode then the small column ran the additional risk in attempting to fight with their scarcity of rifles. Shotguns would indeed, if well concentrated, replace a mine at the initial volley if the men were steady. Troops or police in movement were helpless if either came into the fire of a machine gun, which would spray in a hit or miss cone, regardless of aim or if grenades were used as their wide radius of bursting metal could cover a difficult target. It was the first concentrated volley that would count before the vehicle halted. After that the offensive could quickly pass to the British unless the site selected exposed them to their hidden antagonists.

There were two drawbacks to all this planning. One was, as Connolly had found out already, that there was no efficient intelligence service in the Leitrim Brigade. Ballinamore had a few good men who could remain on in the town unsuspected, but this was the exception. There were lashings of information to be gathered in if the ingathering was systematic. A great number of firesides were really an information centre to a man with an ear, which could direct a pen later. At night time the neighbours in town and in country would drop in all during the autumn and winter nights for card playing or for talk. That chat around the turf was a synthesis of happenings, reported conversations, stray and apt observation and an analysis of enemy movement, and even of intention. Most people were deeply concerned about the young men of their area. Cross webs in relationships, where third and fourth cousins on either side of a house counted in family kinship, would promote interest, but in general there was a protective sympathy and a vigorous awareness of any danger to fighting men. Indeed, danger was more often shared by the non-fighting people who had to work their land and face up to what would happen to them when a column left an area when a fight was finished. The intelligence service in

Leitrim was a leaking battery of information from the want of a competent and thorough staff synthesis of what went on under the people's eyes and very little went on that was not already summed up by the people themselves.

In a town, the military and the RIC would be safeguarded either by the nature of the people around them if they were British Loyalists and *shoneens*, or by their own strength if the people were hostile. In a town, constabulary and military drank, shopped, went to the post office, used telephones, visited friendly houses and mixed somewhat with the people. The railway station was used for heavy stores of food supplies and clothing. Lorries came through, stopped for a while and went on again. Prisoners and hostages in tenders handcuffed or tied up, halted for a night and might be beaten up in the RIC or military barracks. Police went out with military, Auxiliaries and Tans to show them how to get to houses, which were difficult enough to reach even with knowledge, and they then identified unknown men taken in raids. There was the inconsequential aspect in which drunken Crown forces would beat civilians with whips or throw them into nearest rivers.

All this passing panorama was concentrated more sharply in a town, but seldom enough was it put on paper, so that the nearest company captain could study the systematic movement and changing distribution of the forces pitted against his area, and pass it on at once to his battalion. In the country enemy forces were never at leisure or off their guard, as they were in towns. Their very presence on an unfrequented road was an immediate menace to that neighbourhood. Each Volunteer was a potential intelligence feeler as was every RIC man, but the RIC constable made it his routine and deliberate business to gather and access information.

That had been his training since he had left the Depot in the Phoenix Park, and it had now been so thoroughly conditioned that it was a reflex.

The military had a more detached viewpoint because their training had led them to be able to fight other people trained much as they were trained, whose psychology their staffs could appreciate quickly. The army was an avenue for promotion. It could encourage the sense of glory, and add an experience of new country and strange peoples. It was part of army existence to put up with losses. There would always be a core left to pass on the battalion tradition. In this thinly disguised war against country cowboys and town louts who would not meet them in the open, they went out in armoured Lancia, speeding tenders or in well extended patrols. It was disturbing for a regular officer who did not understand the political or psychological reality of what he refused to credit was a foreign country, and whose political outlook was that of an English Tory.

The privates whose understanding of their human surroundings was warped by the misinformation pumped into them by their own propaganda were usually indifferent. They wanted to live their own lives such as was lived in this military vacuum. Their rarefied existence, without decision, was bounded by officers, sergeant majors, sergeants and unconfined by women, drink and contacts with civilians. Their release from authority was now being restricted as the struggle progressed and that kept them closer to the barracks than they desired, but their post had now become a necessary but undesirable protection.

The sense of personal danger and his own mentality, the nearness to pensionable age and the number of his dependants, slights suffered from a hostile or indifferent population, his lack of popularity among the young women, all contributed to enhance the feeling of isolation, or develop the bitterness of the individual constabulary man. This bitterness could be fed by slights, by the growth in popularity of his known opponents and by their elusiveness. It could be added to by the propaganda which the British spread about the IRA, who were well-paid looters, murderers and robbers. The police boycott ordered by Án Dáil had made its pressure felt in his own home area among his parents and relations, from whom he was practically cut off. But the RIC man of Irish birth had a sense of reality about the situation which the British military lacked.

The second drawback was the lack of training in action of the brigades which Seán Connolly was organising. In one way or another minor Volunteer pressure had to be kept up by raiding mails for information, cutting telegraphs and telephone wires, raiding trains for military equipment supplies and for Belfast goods, which were boycotted, trenching roads to confine movement or to injure the springs so that progress was a bone-shaking experience for its occupants, and a continual strain on the undercarriage of the vehicle. In addition there was the watching of potential spies or loyalists, the arresting of lawbreakers and guarding them, carrying out the decrees of Dáil Éireann. Also there was the more dangerous duty of scouting for an enemy approach, the protection of officers and of columns and the sniping of posts. All of these activities made use of Volunteer organisation and enabled it through use to become smooth and adaptable. Orders would be easier to be carried out through practice, while staff work would develop so as to concentrate the effort of this round of organisation effort. This minor work, which should have been routine, would have made for continual handling of men and would lead more effectively to attacks on patrols, vehicles and posts, and on individuals who were giving information.

Sometimes the psychology induced by failure could count as an asset. Even if an attack on a patrol or on a lorry failed, the fact that the formation or movement had been observed and that unseen men could know the enemy pattern and disposition in a district, and that it could be fired on out of a seemingly empty countryside, could upset the morale of constabulary or of military. Their next movement, on foot, or by bicycle, or with lorry, would lead them to observe more carefully and to doubt the presence of possible attackers in the most unlikely places until the doubt could change to strain. The local RIC with their knowledge and sense of proportion could often bring the surrounding menace into perspective provided no new factor such as a visiting column or a strange officer such as Connolly intruded, but they could only solve the proposition for themselves. The military, Tan and Auxiliaries who fought an unreal enemy could not be consoled by the understanding of the RIC. There was of course the solace of drink as a factor. It would work alright, but it disturbed the aim, and its after effects could develop the use of an easy trigger finger more partial to the unoffending.

If a brigade had begun to fight in 1920, it would have gained a certain experience by 1921, and with experience would come confidence and a further security in planning. Then as the fighting on either side became more ruthless, men who were extra-determined about taking chances would grow inured to risk. The people in an area where a stiff resistance was being made took on some of the courage of the fighting men, became more accustomed to the resultant raids and to the round-ups. These were carefully planned on map squares in the security of a barracks. Units were given sectors to move across but it is impossible to search on foot over a small area of land unless troops are a few yards apart. There is cover from view in what seem a very open field and large tracts of bog, and marshy land are very difficult or impossible to cross in wet weather and insecure even after a dry spell. Usually these sweeps provided a mixed bag in which there were no wanted men. In one sense an active area could better protect a countryside than could an inactive area. The British knew they could travel through weak or hesitant country with impunity, and their developing ruthlessness would have a greater effect on men who were unorganised or cowed by their carefully planned reprisals.

Sir Henry Wilson had made numerous crisp remarks at Cabinet meetings during 1920 about the reprisals carried out by RIC, Tans and Auxiliaries. He did not mention soldiers, as it seems that their unorthodox activities were not underlined for his notice by the military authorities in Ireland but before December he was aware of their participation. The Cabinet was divided in its belief and in its responsibility for reprisals. David Lloyd George and Sir Hamar Greenwood were in favour of burning towns usually at nighttime. Winston Churchill had justified reprisals, but towards the end of the year, he considered that the imposition of martial law would have more important results.

The night burning was meant to induce terror and to make the townspeople a substitute for the crudities of the Crown forces instead of the IRA. It was used deliberately as a policy to chastise, not the men who had carried out an operation in the vicinity, but the people who had voted to elect Republicans to parliamentary seats and to place them in power on county, urban and district councils. Raiding parties searched bars and public houses for drink and for money. When spirits had made their actions seem gayer to them, houses and shops were looted and destroyed by petrol projected by sprayers. The inhabitants ran the gauntlet of their drunken mood while they made for safety to the countryside or to houses unconnected with any movement. Lorries, piled high with a miscellaneous treasure trove, from drink to underwear, carried back the reward of effort to the distant barracks.

The *Weekly Summary*, a printed news sheet, was circulated to all RIC and Auxiliary posts. It advocated the strong hand, and advised on expedients such as the shooting of sympathisers if no one else of importance could be discovered in the neighbourhood when an attack had taken place. The officials in Dublin Castle had always hoped that guerilla tactics could be beaten by one method or another, which were tried in a succession of failures. Castle reports to the British Cabinet were optimistic. It was always a question of time with them, but the extension in time received severe jolts when successful column activities impinged on their solutions or on their previous hopeful reports. There is no doubt that the Cabinet was led to believe that a small gang of men were responsible for activity and that the people were hostile to them. When these men had been captured or eliminated the British government could again function in safety throughout the country. The Cabinet, who were responsible for the campaign of unauthorised reprisals, hoped that by these methods active resistance would be curbed or crushed. They refused, however, to take responsibility for the acts of the forces under their control. They hoped this procedure would break the unity of endeavour, and with success in mind the ends to be adopted could be justified. They were determined to reinforce the RIC with ex-soldiers and ex-officers and to make the fighting seem as if police, upholders of law and order, were being attacked by armed bands. Police to the English meant county police who were unarmed and respected, and who were an easygoing part of the rural life and urban life, which co-operated with them to track down lawbreakers. There was no armed constabulary in Great Britian. The nearest conception to such a force would be book knowledge from Russian novels.

Sir Henry Wilson was aware of the tension under which the military lived and acted. He was afraid that indiscipline would develop among the troops if regiments were allowed to carry out individual acts of reprisal for the loss of their men. He was strongly in favour of martial law for the entire country. That would unify the method of control and repression and give additional power to army officers. Reprisals would now be carried out in daylight under military control. Press reports could be more thoroughly censored and the movements of newspaper correspondents be restricted so that their information would not reach friendly or outraged

channels in England or in other parts of the world. The Chief of
the Imperial General Staff strongly recommended shooting by
roster, but he was unwilling to use the full power of the soldiery,
unless the English people agreed to that use of force.

By the end of January 1921 all Munster was under martial law,
and County Kilkenny had been added to the list. The only difference military control made was that men were shot in Cork instead
of being hanged in Dublin. In the martial law area military, all three
types of police shot people when they raided houses and killed
prisoners whom they were escorting to barracks under the plea
that they were trying to escape. This had been the procedure before
martial law was established, and it now diminished the number of
formal official executions by the publicity given to its ceremony,
affecting the entire country simultaneously.

Each month of 1921 meant a further demand of reinforcements
to strengthen the Tans and Auxiliaries as a result of numerous
resignations from the RIC. General Macready, the Commander in
Chief, was steadily demanding additional troops. By March, Wilson
felt that the best method of countering the activity of flying columns
was to stop all transports so that rebels would have to move on foot,
then fan out troops in successive drives backed by their transports.
The British would first have to evacuate troops from Malta, Eygpt,
Silesia, Constantinople and the Rhine. Possibly the Field Marshal
may have been thinking of South Africa where he had served for a
while. There farms had been burned belonging to leaders and men
in Boer commands or in the vicinity of a neighbourhood where
railway telegraph wires had been cut. Crops were destroyed, cattle
and horses driven off land, women and children segregated in
camps where 14,000 children died of disease.

In Leitrim the picking out of the men for Connolly's columns
was eagerly watched by those yet left to be selected. All of them
wanted to be with him for he had raised the hopes of these lads who

were mainly from the countryside. They had come from their farms and that strange world of precision and concentrated attention which went with military awareness was not theirs by nature or through the haphazard training they had so far received. The two columns were ready.[3] Seán Mitchell, the brigadier, had charge of one, and the men under his command watched the swarthy face of the other man, Seán Connolly, his dark eyes that laughed at them a goodbye. 'We'll meet, please God, soon again, lads', he said, as he spread out his section in protective formation. They went off to the east of the county towards the Shannon, intending to attack transport on the roads, or to lie in wait for reinforcements, which might come out to strengthen a garrison on which a feint attack had been made.

A patrol of RIC came out from Drumshanbo fairly regularly to the railway station which was close to the foot of Lough Allen. It was usually not well strung out as this lake side was a quiet backend of country below the southeastern shadow of Slieve Anierin. There were two sweet cans loaded with broken scrap charged with gelignite and connected up by wires to the dynamos of threshers. These were placed on the road beneath the wall of the Protestant cemetery. Inside among the graves were Seán Mitchell and Michael Geoghegan, 20 yards apart, armed with revolvers and grenades, ready to blow the cans. Further up towards the railway gates Tom O'Reilly, Mattie Boylan and the captain of Drumshanbo company stood with their rifles. They had waited there in a tense night silence when slight sounds seem to amplify themselves and even the absence of sound takes on a quality of noise. Suddenly they heard the noise of regular boot thuds on the road. The patrol was moving towards them, talking to each other and close together judging by their noise. The darkness and the tension made the sounds seem as loud as the heartbeats of the men who waited. The RIC patrols passed by the churchyard and then moved on past the second section of riflemen, but there was no explosion. The orders were to open fire as soon as they heard the detonation of the mines. The three men wondered what had happened, but they waited for the police on their return. They had counted over 20 police as they passed up. The patrol came back, but again no sound came from the graveyard, nor had the police noticed either the sweet tins or the cable which were yet on the roadside.

When the sound of feet had deadened, a disconsolate group of men gathered on the roadside near the mines. They had failed for some reason which they could not understand. The brigadier with his other mine operator went off at once to inform Connolly of the failure. They found him close to Garvagh where he had held an ambush position. He examined the cable and detonators. The detonators had failed to explode because they had been wrongly wired.

That same evening of 2 March Seán MacEoin had been captured in Mullingar as he was coming back by train from Dublin. J. J. Brady, a Longford commandant, was on the same train. He saw his brigade vice-commandant being questioned on the platform, and then handcuffs were snapped on to his wrists. On his way to the barracks MacEoin made a wild dash, but he did not know the town sufficiently well, nor did he meet friends, and he was wounded and recaptured. 'Beef to the heels like a Mullingar heifer' should have been the proud slogan of the town. In practically any other town in the Midlands MacEoin might have been able to slip into an open door, where he would have found friendly people, or a door might have suddenly been pushed back for him, but this garrison town minded its own business, and its business was to make money from cattle men who held the best fattening ground in Ireland. Brady brought on word to the brigade, and it was forwarded to Connolly. Seamus Conway had gone into Mullingar to pick up what information he could find. Connolly was distressed. As a result of the many ranks MacEoin had held there were now three positions to be filled. Connolly felt that an attempt should be made at once to rescue the prisoner in Mullingar. He selected Leitrim men who were anxious to assist. They were to join with the Longford men, but the British interrupted the planning by removing MacEoin in an ambulance to the capital. Dublin men had been waiting on the road towards Lucan, but the escort did not pass by the Dublin men who had been trained in close quarter fighting in their own city.

Two days after the mine failure at Drumshanbo the section was to wait for the British near the chapel at Gowel, six miles northeast of Carrick. Two of them had, the previous evening, just missed a patrol of ten Tans at Kilclara, who had come out to collect the mail at the post office. They felt secure enough in this western part of the county to send out small patrols on routine work, but the use of such armed strength proved that even the collection of mail was a matter for an escort. Connolly had discussed the plan of action before this section had moved away from him. Word of the section movements was passed on in such a way that it was meant to be listened to by friends of the Plucker Gallagher in order that it would reach his long ears. The lads were supposed to attend mass in the morning at Gowel chapel to receive holy communion, as it was the first Friday of the month. The 'Plucker' was heard to make inquiries about the possibility of the lads attending the chapel. The 'Plucker' who was a sergeant was fond of taking a fat turkey or a goose for the boys when he was raiding with Tans or military. It was easy enough then to wring the neck of a succulent bird, for no complaint against an RIC man would be listened to at either the local barracks or at the county headquarters. As Leitrim was prolific in turkeys and in geese the 'Plucker's' aching stomach could be amply satisfied in the countryside.

Mass was to have been at eight o'clock. The column expected that a strong body of troops might turn up for the raid. The men put up at Keonbrook, and there were ten of them. Early next morning they were on their way towards a selected position when they heard the sound of heavy cars, and as they lay down they watched the mixed convoy of RIC and military pass down towards the chapel. They were more numerous than they had expected. There could be little hope of capturing the convoy on its way back as the ground was not suitable, but they decided they would pick off as many of them as they could before they left or were driven from their hill view. The Military and RIC divided the men and women as they left the chapel after Mass, into two groups for searching. Women searchers often went around with the Tans and military. They were attached usually to the RIC barracks where they served in more than one capacity. That morning some of the Volunteers had been warned not to attend Mass. The RIC and Bedfords made insulting remarks and directed threats to the men and boys whom they pushed around as they searched for arms in their pockets and for concealed information in their minds. The women searchers fumbled at the clothes of the indignant women and girls, whose opinion of their character was loudly and unequivocally asserted. Soon, the searchers moved off, baffled. They could be seen from the side of Sheemore, the fairy haunted mountain whose caves concealed a great number of fairies.

The men lay on one side behind a stone wall some 300 yards from the road, but that was the only cover they could find which had a view along the roadside. Below them were the openings of the fairy caves and behind was a bare rise of ground over which it would be difficult enough to withdraw later. From their position they heard the motor start up noisily in the frosty air. There was a waggonette followed by a private car, then the Black Maria, a military lorry and a touring car. The six rifles picked out the drivers and grouped on the two large vehicles when they had come into the rifle sights within their position. The rear car reversed and was able to get out of the line of fire. Military and police tumbled out behind the road ditch, but the police were quicker at getting cover. There

were a few crack shots in this small section of the column, and the
rest of those who had rifles happened to be fairly good marksmen.
The British tried to move up along a wall to one flank but good
marksmanship made them undecided and hesitant. After a time a
party moved under what cover they could find along a low stone
wall, but an officer who was making use of his field glasses to
observe movement, and to estimate the range, was wounded. In the
distance at long range a policeman was hit as he tried to get into a
house. The section remained in their position for over an hour,
then they crawled up the slope slowly exposed to the fire of the
mixed force.

The estimate of losses by the British varied. A boy whom the
military met near the roadside further on was taken into the lorry,
and in press gang fashion he was made to guide them by a back road
into Carrick, because they wanted to avoid the main roads. When
he came home he said that all the soldiers in the lorry in which he
travelled were lying on the floor wounded and that blood dripped
out at the end from the moaning men. The official report gives a
little information:

A party of military and police were ambushed at Sheemore . . . as a
result of the attack Lt Wilson and four men of the Bedfordshire
Regiment and two RIC, Sergeant Healy and Constable Costello, were
wounded. Lt. Wilson and some of his men were seriously wounded
and the police but slightly. . . It is stated that the party were in search
for 'wanted' men, believed to be in the district. A large force of RIC
and Auxiliaries, with some military, proceeded to the district, and
detachments from surrounding stations are also in the locality, where a
general search is being made . . . One of the Ford cars used by the
Crown forces showed striking evidence of the attack in the form of
countless bullets. Many people have left the district fearing reprisals . . .
Lt. Wilson died of wounds. The attacking party is estimated at close

on one hundred. The survivors among the Crown forces declare the marksmanship was most deadly.

Evidently the fairies must have strengthened the small group of riflemen. Fairy darts would probably carry a long distance, and they would surely be accurate. Maybe a Leitrim prototype of Garret the Earl, whose silver-shod horse goes the rounds of Lough Gur, and who wakes every so many years to inquire in a rumbling voice from his cavern if the time had come to fight for Ireland, may also have helped the section. But fairies being as jealous as humans they must have felt indignant when their proud effort was not even mentioned in the official British report. As usual the enemy had scorned the unseen influence, which, in Irish history, had made alliance with strength and determination.

The concentration of troops, Auxiliaries and RIC, surprised at this activity in a quiet spot, were aggressive and overbearing in their raids, interrogations and destruction. Houses were burned close to Carrick, and a creamery near the chapel of Gowel, while the people left empty houses behind as if a famine had again struck this quiet countryside. The search continued its wide net which the column avoided, but Frank Davis on a journey into Leitrim to find Seán Connolly had barely time to fling himself over a hedge before a dust swarm of Auxiliaries swept over where he had been. He was not able to see Connolly owing to the enemy activity in the east of the county, but the message which he brought with him was sent on at once. The Longford men wanted Connolly to return to take charge of the Longford flying column. He sent back word for the column to keep somewhere around Columcille area which was a very staunch fallback for them and that he would be back to them within a week. He had yet work to do in Leitrim.

Near Fenagh, Connolly's section of his column lay in position for eight hours on a chilly March day for a patrol of from ten to

fifteen RIC which went between Mohill and Ballinamore, sometimes cycling, other times in a lorry. As the chill crept into his
bones Connolly whispered to Bernie Sweeney: 'Have you a drop of
the holy water for I'm perished.' He was handed a naggin bottle
from which he took a good swig. The patrol had some other
thought in their heads that day for they did not come that way.
Some nights later Connolly, Sweeney, Seamus Maguire, Michael
Baxter and Andy McPartland went into Ballinamore to wait for a
patrol. They were able to take cover in a disused house to avoid
standing around, but after a long wait they had to leave the town.

The reunited column met again near Attymus where they
talked about their adventures and their failures. The men in
Mitchell's column, who had hoped to be picked by Connolly when
he selected his column, were now somewhat more content as
they had one action to their credit, Sheemore. Both half columns
expected that something would happen when they had been brought
together. This planning, which they now looked forward to, saved
them from the boredom of inaction, which too often engendered
indifference and inefficiency. Heavy mines, weighing close on 200
pounds weight had been brought down from Aughnasheelin, and
the men sensed they might soon be used.

Connolly had decided to inspect the road between Carrick and
Mohill, and as a guide he picked out Frank McKeown who knew
the district well. Between Mohill and Drumsna, beyond Drumcree
Mills, Connolly saw a position which he thought would suit. A low
lying road ran below a hill from which it could be raked by fire from
a good distance. Close by was thin light wood which would give
cover to the men while they waited. With an ample use of scouts
the column would be saved the strain of waiting in their firing
positions, for a long wait took the edge off alertness. He could use,
he estimated, about thirty men on this hillside. McKeown and
himself tested the selected ground thoroughly from every angle of

view of men lying in position, and every possibility of chance and mischance was calculated in the proposed attack on a lorry or two coming from either direction. A trench would have to be dug for a mine, which would deal with the first lorry, and the road surface would have to be carefully replaced and tramped down to avoid suspicion. When Connolly had mapped the site carefully he knew where he could best make use of his men. If the mine worked, one lorry would be disorganised or out of action quickly and that would permit of more concentrated fire on the second lorry. The Mills were on the main road from Carrick to Mohill and there was always daily military traffic on it.

The two men returned to Attymus that night satisfied with their detailed reconnaissance, their minds full of the impending ambush. Frank MacKeown went to bed, but Connolly wandered off to inspect the charges, connections and mines to make sure that everything was in good working condition as the column had been mobilised for four the next morning. Within an hour Connolly returned, but he was upset. The mines had crumpled to pieces in his hands when he had examined them, and again he knew that his plans were also crumbling. Evidently the sand from Dernaheltra was responsible for the mishap. It was not suitable for mixing with the cement, and the weight of the broken metal had not served to reinforce the case. Up to this he had had a good many mishaps. The Leitrim men had been eager and willing to serve his instructions, and this ambush, if successful, would have been his last in the county for some time to come. He had promised the Longford column that he would return to it. He was anxious to get back to a well-armed unit, which had been training itself in action.

The column was on parade early in the morning. It was time for it to move for it had been a while in the neighbourhood, but the men, who had been expecting from the undercurrent of excitement which had gushed up in their thoughts that they would be called upon to prepare to fight that day, were disappointed. The column was again split up. Mitchell and his men started off for Deffier, near the Shannon canal a few miles to the south of Drumshanbo. Around this post they were to wait for patrols. Connolly had told Bernie Sweeney to take charge of the remaining men, eleven in all, five of whom had rifles. They were to move along through Funshinagh towards Garvagh. They had small mines with them, weighing about two stone each.

Connolly had hopes that he might carry out an ambush that day, and as he walked along he selected a thatched house near a bridge. That would suit for a mine position, he thought. At about half past eight the column came across the brow of a hill overlooking Selton Lake and the marshy land beneath. They passed by William Latimer's house as they went down; then they made their way up by the lake edge to two houses, McCullough's and Flynn's. McCullough's and Latimer's were Orange houses. The men who were sent to McCullough's were refused food, but they took it, and they made the family cook for them. Then a guard of two men who were relieved at intervals was placed on this house which was further in than Flynn's and about 100 yards from it, to keep it under observation.

There were nine men in Charlie Flynn's house. Some of them lay down, but Connolly and the Brigade Vice-Commandant Wrynn went off to inspect a position. If any lorries passed on towards Ballinamore that day Connolly intended that the small column would wait for them as they were on their way back. Bernie Sweeney went up to a house on the side of the hill, on the road verge to talk to Mrs Murphy. Soon they had drifted in talk back to Lord Leitrim and to the other landlords who had held this countryside firmly under their heels. Leitrim was a boyo whose conduct was execrable and strange enough to the quiet norm of life there but for legends to be woven about him and his seigniorial misdemeanours.

The road from Garvagh went uphill beyond Murphy's, then went down steadily and from the road the bare edge of Selton Lake could be seen below and to the left. Wide deep drains carried off the water from the soggy bottoms, where there were no hedges. What hedges there were on the rise were slight and the sparsity of early spring opened out the view through them. There were a few low banks and some small amount of cover a few hundred yards away from the road, where the rounding of the slope cut off the view slightly. Below that again the bottom lands could be seen and the eye was not restricted by banks or quicks as the land slanted upwards to a crest some eight hundred yards away. This seemed a strange valley for a small column to rest in. There were hostile Orangemen beside them, no chance of escape across the valley or to the west and no way up to the road in case of trouble. There were no sentries posted towards the roadside, and the two men who were on watch were there for the purpose of preventing the McCulloughs from leaving their house.

The Master, Charlie Flynn, came back from his scholars for his dinner at half past three. He found the men, whom he had seen from out a back window winding down by Latimer's in the morning as he had left for school, in his house. Most of them he knew for he was a noted footballer, but he had never before met with Seán Connolly. When the Master had finished his dinner, he was looking at the mines and was being given an explanation of their use when word came in suddenly through his brother, James Flynn, who had gone out to the road with a plough, that a shot had been heard from the direction of Garvagh Cross. The men had finished their dinner, and one of them, Joe Beirne, was shaving. Some of the men said that if the British were coming for them they would take extra precautions to come quietly, and if that was their intention they would see that no shot was fired. Besides, they knew lorries came frequently along the road over the hill to

Ballinamore. Later on it was found that a policeman on the raiding party had fired a shot. He was attempting to give the column men information of their approach, and his rifle was the only means he now had of sending on a warning, yet that warning had not been correctly interpreted. Connolly ordered the men to pack up their kit, examine their weapons and be ready to leave the house as soon as he would hear more definite information. He asked Master Flynn to go up to the roadway to have a look around and see if there was any movement on the road or on the far side of it. It was past four o'clock when Flynn reached the road, but he could not see anyone there. He walked up towards the height of ground from which Garvagh Cross would be visible, but before he reached the rise he heard the sound of a lorry. He crossed in over the road-bank and from there he signalled back with his hand to inform some of the men who were to have been watching him from the house, that there was danger. Then, thinking that the lorry was the ordinary passing lorry of troops, he went up towards it for it had halted outside of McCullough's gate. A police officer, Thomas Gore-Hickman,[4] the RIC District Inspector in Mohill, got out of a car which was behind the soldiers and walked over to Flynn:

'Did you see any armed men around here', he asked?

'No, I didn't, I was at school all day and I've just come back.'

'But you should have seen them', said the District Inspector abruptly, 'and you should have known they were about here.'

To the British officer the District Inspector said: 'We'll search these two houses here.'

Soldiers went down the narrow sunken lane which dropped towards McCullough's. The District Inspector took charge of some soldiers. He put Flynn in front of him, and the group went down towards the house in which Connolly and the column had been left. The remaining soldiers spread out behind the road bank which overlooked the further distance. A Lewis gunner set his tripod on the pier of the gate. The Master, who had seen these preparations, now knew the column men were in a trap. He wondered what had happened to them and then thought of what would happen to himself. When the first shot came from any of the column men, he expected to get a bullet in the back from Gore-Hickman, who had his Webley in his hand, behind him. The column men had at least some minutes to arrange themselves to face the advancing danger, but Flynn was without any defence or hope as he walked forward.

Rifle fire began before the soldiers came to Flynn's house. The military on the road must have seen some movement of the column men below them through the bushes. The first raiding party on its way to McCullough's hearing the shooting turned towards the east in the direction of the back of Flynn's house. The District Inspector and his following went on towards the bottom land while the Master was brought into his own kitchen, a prisoner, under the guard of one of the Bedfords.

While Flynn was walking up towards the road, men were getting their equipment ready. Bernie Sweeney went out of the house from the side which faced the road, but he could not hear any engine sound. Sometimes a hill which has hollows on either side of it plays tricks with sound. He went back to tell Seán Connolly that there was no sign of any British troops in front. Connolly had moved the men out to a small shrubbery of blackthorns behind which they had a little cover. Purple buds were numerous on the thick-set branches. To one side there was a deep red flame from upthrust willow branches. Spring was in the air and around their feet with its sense of birth and fulfilment. Sweeney who had a pair of field glasses swung them on to the road-bank, and it was then he first saw a khaki movement. They had evidently been there, the soldiers, when he had gone out in front of the house to observe. His rifle was now in McCullough's with one of the men who had been posted on guard duty there. Seán Connolly used the field glasses.

'We'd best split up', he said to Sweeney, 'we're too many men together and there's no cover that I can see. You take three or four of the lads and try to get towards the North.'

He turned around as he spoke. From where he lay behind the butts of thorn the ground lower down the valley did not look as exposed as it actually was. Away towards the North was the high slate-blue ridge of Slieve Anierin looking down on the quiet valleys. The dark green of rushes stood out against a background of shrivelled yellow-grey grass, and in the marshy ground the flat blades of iris angled stiffly. None of the men on the column knew the neighbourhood. The North lay up by Latimer's on the far side of the valley along the line they had come down that morning.

Sweeney took Captain John Joe O'Reilly, Michael Baxter, Joe Beirne and Andy McPartland further down into the bottom land, under slight cover. Fifty yards away he could see Wrynn and John Joe O'Reilly. Three of Sweeney's men had rifles or carbines and as they made use of them the Lewis gun began its sharp, unnerving bursts. Rifle fire seemed to come from the road bank further down the hill. Sweeney borrowed a rifle from Joe Beirne, and as he stood behind a tree he sighted it carefully but he could not see any of the advancing soldiers who were making good use of banks and odd bushes. The two enemy parties from McCullough's and Flynn's were trying to cut across towards the bottom land. He swung the rifle up on to the road bank and fired a few shots.

Young John Joe O'Reilly was wounded when, as they were close to a boggy drain, they ran across the open and while they ran bullets from the Lewis cut the ground in front of them and behind them. They were moving across the line of fire and that made an apt target for the gunner. Baxter and Beirne sprawled forward, wounded, then Sweeney was hit in the groin. He could not move with the pain, but he could hear the bullet noises as they went over him. Soldiers passed close by, but they must have thought he was either dead or seriously wounded. Below him as the khaki soldiers moved onwards he saw Baxter and Beirne now on their hands and knees trying to move, but as the soldiers came to them they bashed their heads with the butt end of rifles and stood over their moans until they lay flatly sprawled.

Sweeney crawled on to a drain behind him, his will making his arms pull his body after him. It was a deep drain, and the cold water shocked him into alertness and covered him to his chin. He put his rifle under him as his eyes followed the khaki figures searching through the level ground. As he watched he heard a crash of bursting grenades. He turned his head to find out what this new menace meant, and as he angled he saw Captain John Joe O'Reilly pull the pin from a hand grenade, but as he stretched out his arm to throw it, he fell backwards with a sudden jump, wounded.

The soldiers who had been searching further down towards the lake came back. They were now looking for Sweeney who was drinking the drain water to cool his thirst. He was trying to keep his senses together so as not to slip down into the water. The Bedfords looked around from the landmark of the quiet bodies, but they could not see their quarry who lay against the soft bank up to his nose in water. They swore at him and cursed in their soldiers' way at each other, then he could hear their voices moving away uphill while they halted to rest from the weight of the bodies they were swinging between them. They would probably come back again to search he thought, but his only hope now was the covering cloak which was creeping over the western sky.

Birds low flying and calling to each other in the now hushed indifference of evening mist swung across the lake and back over the tufted grass. They brought in the twilight, and with it came a more welcome sound, the buzz of a lorry, as it began to warm up its engine in the cold air. Sweeney shaped his mouth to whistle, but he was not able to make any sound except grunts of pain. Then he made the skeleton of a shout as he hoisted himself up out of the drain. An old woman on the opposite hill heard him, and some of the local lads who were searching for survivors and for weapons came across to him. They carried him up to a slated house, Murphy's, lower down the Ballinamore road. The household did what they could for his wound, but he was anxious to get away from the Selton Lake district which he felt would be raided thoroughly next day.

McPartland had already come to the house Sweeney was in. He had tried to drag the wounded John Joe O'Reilly with him, but he had to leave him behind. Then crawling under cover he got beyond the military flank to safety. That night Sweeney was taken away in a horse and trap, but the people nearby were frightened. A wounded man meant for them not a feeling of compassion, but the terror of what would happen if he was found in their house. The place might be burned over their heads, and their men shot in the presence of their women if Sweeney was caught there, and they refused sanctuary. He remembered, however, there was a man, Dr P. J. Dolan,[5] who lived near Ballyduff and who was on his lone. Dr Dolan welcomed him and looked after his wounds, and he was then sent up into the mountains where all the neighbours were as staunch as the mountain heights.

The two men[6] who had been on guard at McCullough's house got down towards the lake with their two rifles. They hid in a dyke, and it is said Gore-Hickman and RIC men passed by them, but one of them would not allow the other to fire on the District Inspector. They lay there for a while, left their rifles behind them, and escaped. Sweeney's rifle was recovered later as was Captain John Joe O'Reilly's revolver which was close by his body. When Gore-Hickman, accompanied by a British officer, came back to Flynn's house from the bottom, he was excited by the killing which he had been in on and that probably saved the house from the expected flames. He struck Master Flynn repeatedly with his fist and with a revolver butt on the chin. He took him outside the back door where he threatened to shoot him for leading himself and the military into an ambush. While he was bullying his prisoner, blankets were taken from the house to make it easier for the soldiers to carry up the bodies. There were five of them, and they comprised Brigade Vice-Commandant Wrynn, Adjutant Beirne, Captain John Joe O'Relly and the other John Joe O'Reilly and Michael Baxter. Jack Hunt, whose house on the road near Carrick had been recently burned out, received a severe leg wound and Connolly was badly wounded.[7] None of their captors paid any attention to the wounded, as was the custom with both military and police then. Some of the bodies were flung into the lorry but a few were piled into the back of Gore-Hickman's car. Connolly was thrown into the lorry like a sack of flour, and he moaned from pain. The District Inspector was anxious to get away before the darkness would blur his line of vision. To the British the crawling night light was a menace. It cut them off from their strong barracks, and it dulled the accuracy of their weapons. More particularly, on this night they were anxious to put distance between them and the blood soaked slopes, for maybe that strange telepathic information which they associated with the IRA might be ahead of them on their journey. The darkness was otherwise to the home-based Volunteers. It was a cover and a friendly shield.

When the lorry reached Mohill Barracks, Connolly asked for a drink of water, but no one would offer him a drink. 'Piss in his mouth, that's good enough for him,' said an RIC man as he leaned over the side of the lorry. Then as they set out for Carrick, the soldiers shouted 'Fresh meat, fresh meat', in imitation of a huxter's cry, while the District Inspector's parting shout was: 'We'll salt them down.' That indeed was close enough to historical procedure. Many the head of an Irish chief salted in brine had been sent on in a firkin to add to the adornment of a Dublin Castle spike, and in later days many a Tory head had been preserved to gratify the Cromwellian planters. The Bedfords were in good humour. They had revenged the shot which had killed an officer[8] of their regiment six days ago and had compensated for the numerous wounded at Sheemore. Another regiment, the East Yorks, shared in the victory. Some of the rifles which had been found on the dead had been rifles which that regiment had surrendered about nine months ago. Their men had been suddenly held up at Corrawallen, six miles away from Selton Lake, as they were guarding a broken-down lorry which had been removing bedding from an RIC barracks.

The official report added interesting information: 'The remarkable statement is made that the attackers were all dressed in the same way – dark-green breeches and trenchcoats, while they also had military equipment.' The military headquarters account of the affair is: 'A party of the 1st Bedford and Hampshire Regiment were ambushed about six miles north of Mohill. An engagement ensued in which the troops assaulted the rebels' position and in a running fight shot 6 of them dead.' Another account states:

> A mixed patrol of military and RIC were attacked by 30 or 40 men who emerged from houses on the side of the road and took to trenches carefully prepared for an ambush. Fire was opened by the Crown forces who brought in a Lewis gun. A battle of a fierce character ensued. Bombs were used by the Crown forces and the attackers who replied with bombs also used service rifles.

When the lorry reached Carrick-on-Shannon, Jack Hunt had to jump down from it on his wounded leg and walk to his cell in the county jail, which was held by military. Next day he and Master Flynn were seen to by Dr Delaney of Carrick who dressed Hunt's wound and who was kind to both of them. Connolly lasted until noon the next day. He refused to give his name, and he would not answer any of his questioners. A medical officer of the Bedfords stationed in Boyle remarked later in a shop in that town: 'The bravest man I ever saw was that young man Connolly. He wouldn't allow me to look after his wounds because I was in uniform.' Father Dalton[9] and another priest were allowed in to see him as he was dying. One of them was a friend of the Connolly family but Connolly would not tell them who he was. 'Tell my mother I died for Ireland,' he said to them as they left him.

The day Connolly died, Friday 12 March, there was a great fuss about the identification of the bodies.[10] Master Charlie Flynn and Bernie Sweeney's brother, who were in the jail, were taken with other prisoners to look at and name the dead bodies, but no one would admit they knew any of the dead. The British must have had a suspicion that Seán Connolly was among the dead. They brought RIC Constable Josephs, who had been in Ballinalee, and he it was who pointed out Connolly.

The military had not come out by chance that day to Selton Lake as they had been told where to find the column by the neighbours. When some of the men went into McCullough's, hostility met them flatly enough. There was a young son of William Latimer there, aged nine or ten, and he was allowed to leave the house to return across by the lake to his own home. Latimer's mother had died that morning, and he had a good excuse for visiting Mohill that day with his pony and trap.[11] Dr Pentland from Mohill was holding his dispensary a little distance above Garvagh Cross. He had served in the British army and was definitely hostile. He was usually finished with his patients by three o'clock, and Latimer either told him there were armed men in the valley, at the dispensary or in Mohill. Dr Pentland informed the District Inspector and military were sent on from Carrick-on-Shannon.

William Latimer, it appears, was in the habit of visiting George Connor's pub beside the police barracks in Mohill and over the backyard wall he had frequent chats with a red-haired constable, Teigue. Already he had evidently been suspect. A despatch was sent on to GHQ giving particulars about Latimer, but there was a considerable delay before confirmed sentence reached the Leitrim men. Two men in daylight on 30 March went to Latimer's house. He would not open the door for them, nor would he come outside. One of them flung in a hand grenade through a window, but it did not explode. Latimer came out then, and they shot him on his own street. He had two revolvers on him.[12]

Dr Pentland came from Mohill to see Latimer's body. When he returned to Mohill, he packed his bags and went at once to England with his wife and child. There was no information in Leitrim or at GHQ about his new address, but O'Brien of Mohill who was an auctioneer had advertised the sale of his house and furniture. When armed men went into O'Brien's, he gave them Dr Pentland's address in London. It was sent at once to GHQ but the Truce came on in the meantime, and then nothing could be done to Dr Pentland. Some time later while the doctor stood at the door of his London house a heavy truck swerved on the street, came up to the footpath and crushed him to death.[13] Gore-Hickman, the District Inspector, evidently thought Ireland was not a healthy place for him. He suddenly disappeared to England 'on official business', and he remained there until the Truce had been thoroughly tested by others for their safety. Then he returned.

That same day that Seán Connolly died, 12 March, the Longford column thought that he would be back towards their area to command them. Seamus Conway had taken over the column in the meantime. Some of them to keep the British busy and to show that actions could be planned after the arrest of their column commander, Seán MacEoin, went into Granard that night intending to meet a patrol there. They fired on the patrol as it was forming up outside the barracks. The patrol broke up into odd numbers which scattered around the unlighted streets. The column commander ran into a Tan in the dark, and the two men fought with their revolvers. The Tan was wounded and was disarmed. The RIC admitted that three of their number had been wounded that night.

The evening on which Connolly was mortally wounded, the other section of the column, under Seán Mitchell, was about three miles away. They heard the rifle shots and the machine gun like an enraged woodpecker. They thought that it was probably an ambush, but the vagaries of the police or military were so strange that they had often fired away at a memory some six months old as they passed along the roadways. Soon enough the column heard what had happened. The men were despondent and leaderless. The Leitrim Brigade had lost some of its best officers and its new and real driving force, Seán Connolly. Seán Mitchell, its brigadier, was neither active in mind nor in intention, nor would he normally go out of his way to look for a fight.

The new weapons in which the column had been trained, the contact mine, cart box bomb and road mine, were not afterwards made use of in the brigade. The mines which were buried in the roadsides waited for men to explode them against lorries, but no one disturbed their quiet graves. Men tried to carry out minor attacks, but the enemy seemed to be aware, or luck was against the planners.

Later in April when a Tan was killed in Ballinamore, the remaining Tans in the barracks were threatening to burn a number of houses in the town. They had their prepared list ready, but an RIC man, Mugan from Mayo, stood in their way. He refused to allow them to leave the barracks to destroy the houses. He remained on guard with his rifle, but the Tans killed him before he could fire on them. His death saved a few houses and maybe some lives that night.

There were a number of men drawn from the Dublin Brigade who had volunteered to go to county brigades as organisers. In the Typographica, which had once been brigade headquarters in Gardiner Street, they had listened to lectures by Michael Collins, Emmett Dalton, Ginger O'Connell, Eoin Plunkett and myself. Paddy Morrissey from the 4th Dublin Battalion, who had been attending the course, had been selected to go to County Mayo, but his county was later changed to Leitrim. Collins saw him before he left by train with all the necessary credentials and accoutrements of an imaginary commercial traveller. 'You're going in to the most treacherous county in Ireland', he told him, 'so keep a good eye out.' That was cheerful news for an organiser who had never before been in the area, but Morrissey, who kept close to the hills, was able to report by the end of a month that the people whom he had met and with whom he had stayed were as fine a people as he had ever encountered.

In the counties in which Seán Connolly served there are reminders in memory of him.[14] In Mantua, County Roscommon, near where once a contact mine exploded, there is a Seán Connolly Hall. In County Longford the local Ballinalee football team, in the parish of Clonbroney, is now the 'Seán Connollys', and in Ballinamuck where the bastioned barracks stood on guard, there is a high altar built in his memory from money collected through the energy of James J. Brady, the former Commandant of the 5th Battalion, from people of Longford blood in New York. Above Selton Lake at the rise of the hill is a figure of a volunteer in limestone with his head turned in the direction of the bottom land, where Connolly and his comrades met their deaths. Beneath it is an inscription:

Muinntir Liathdroma agus Longphuirt
agus a gclann thar lear san oileán úr
a thóg an leacht seo
i gcuimhne bródamhail ceanamhail
an dreama a bhfuil a n-ainmneacha
gearrtha inntí
a thug a seirbhís go fonnmhar do
Róisín Dubh
agus a d'éag ar son
Poblacht na h-Éireann
a fógruigheadh Lúan Cásca 1916.
Briogaidéir Seán Ó Conghaile
Briogaidéir Séamus Ó Rinn
Ceannphort Seósamh Ó Beirn
Caiptín Mícheál Baicstéir
Caiptín Seán Ó Raghallaigh
Leist Seán S. Ó Raghallaigh

Geobhaimid-ne bás ionnós go mairfidh an
Náisiún Gaedhealach. Déanfaidh ár gcuid fola
an sean tír a áit-bhairteadh agus áit-bheodadh –

                            SEÁN MAC DIARMADA

Translation

Leitrim and Longford people
and their kith and kin overseas in the New World
erected this monument
in proud and loving remembrance
of those whose names
are inscribed thereon
who served Ireland faithfully
and who died for
the Irish Republic
proclaimed on Easter Monday 1916.
Brigadier Seán Connolly
Brigadier Seamus Wrynne
Commandant Joseph Beirne
Captain Michael Baxter
Captain John O'Reilly
Lieut John J. O'Reilly

We will die so that the Irish Nation
may live. Our blood will
revitalise and re-awaken the old land.

SEÁN MCDERMOTT

Republican plot, Clonbroney Chapel, near Ballinalee

APPENDIX I

IRA Command Structures in Leitrim, Longford and Roscommon
January–March 1921

Brigade Staff
O/C   Seán Mitchell, Bernard Sweeney (after May 1921)
VOC   Harry McKeon
Adj.   Joseph Beirne, Eugene Kilkenny (after March 1921)
QM   John Joe O'Reilly, Pat Tiernan (after March 1921)
IO   Charles Pinkman

1st Batt. HQ: Cloone
O/C: Jack (Seán) Briody, John Joe McGarry, Patrick Cosgrave
VOC Johnny Conlon
Adj.   Barney Magee, John Joe Cooney
QM   Johnny Conlon, James Canning
Area: Cloone, Carrigallen, Drumeela, Aughavas, Cornageeha,
        Fearglass, Bornacoola, Drumreilly

2nd Batt. HQ: Ballinamore
O/C   Bernard McGowan, Packy Flynn
VOC   Michael Bohan
Adj.   Michael Baxter
QM   Bernard Sweeney
Area: Ballinamore, Aughnasheelin, Crimlin, Corraleehan, Kilturbrid
        North and South, Drumshanboo, Aughawillan, Fenagh

3rd Batt. HQ: Carrick-on-Shannon
O/C   Peter Murray Frank Rourke
VOC   Patrick Hardigan
Adj.   William Farrell, Gerard Flynn
QM   Joseph Mitchell
Area: Mohill, Carrick, Drumsna, Garvagh, Jamestown, Gowel, Eslin,
         Leitrim, Annaduff

Leitrim IRA local military actions referenced in this memoir

Sept. 1920	burning of Ballinamore Courthouse
Sept. 1920	attack on Mohill Barracks
16 Jan. 1921	attack on Ballinamore Barracks
4 Mar. 1921	Sheemore ambush by flying column (2nd section)
4–10 Mar. 1921	Flying column actions at Drumshambo, Garvagh, Attymus
11 Mar. 1921	Selton Hill ambush of flying column (1st section)

Flying Column (Jan.–Mar. 1921; disbanded after 11 Mar. 1921)
1st Section

O/C   Seán Connolly* (w/c/d)
Men   Michael Baxter*, Joe Beirne*, Paddy Guckian (w/e), Jack Hunt
       (w/c), Pee McDermot (e), Andy McPartand (w/e), Capt. John
       Joe O'Reilly*, John Joe O'Reilly*, Bernie Sweeney (w/e), Seamus
       (James) Wrynn* [c = captured, d = died, e = escaped, * = killed,
       w = wounded]

2nd Section

O/C   Seán Mitchell
Men   Mattie Boyle, Michael Geoghegan, Michael Martin, Harry
       McKeon, Joe Nagle, Thomas O'Reilly

LONGFORD BRIGADE

Brigade Staff HQ: Longford
O/C Tom Reddington (1918), Seán Connolly (1919), John Murphy
VOC Seán Connolly, Seán MacEoin (Nov 1920), Patrick Callaghan
(Mar 1921)
Adj. James Flood, Michael F. Heslin
QM Ned Cooney, Frank Davis
Engineer Eugene Kilbride

1st Batt. HQ: Columcille
O/C Seán MacEoin, replaced by Seán Murphy (Mar 1921)
VOC Seán Connolly (until Nov 1920)
Adj. Seán Duffy
QM Frank Davis
Area: Ballinalee, Edgeworthstown, Granard, Mullinlaghta, Killoe,
Columcille with outposts at Finea, Streete and Rathowen

2nd Batt. HQ: Longford
O/C Michael Murphy
Area: Longford town, Clonguish and Shannon up to Tarmonbarry
including companies in Ferefad, Newtownforbes, Ballycormack

3rd Batt. HQ: Lanesborough
O/C Michael Mulligan
Area: Lanesborough, Ballymahon, Kenagh, Rathcline

4th Batt.
O/C Leo Baxter
Adj. Jack Clancy, Michael Ballesty
Area: Ardagh, Moydow, Legan

5th Batt.

O/C   James J. Brady

VOC   Charles Reynolds

Adj.   James Mulligan

QM   Frank Whitney, Paddy Kiernan

Area: Drumlish, Ballinamuck, Dromard, Moyne

Flying Column

O/C   Seán Connolly, Seán MacEoin (Nov. 1920), Seamus Conway
    (Mar. 1921)

Longford IRA local actions referenced in this memoir

10 May 1917	By-election won by Sinn Féin's Joe McGuinness
June 1920	Ballymahon
20 June 1920	Mostrim
10 July 1920	Ballinamuck
Mid-1920	Smear, near Lana, Field, Lough Gowna
Sept. 1920	Arvagh (Co. Cavan), Ballinalee, Ballinamore (Co. Leitrim), Granard, Top
20 Sept. 1920	Mohill (Co. Leitrim)
12 Dec. 1920	Ballinalee
6 Jan. 1921	Drumlish
Feb. 1921	Clonfin

NORTH ROSCOMMON BRIGADE

Brigade Staff   HQ: Hillstreet

O/C   Seamus Ryan (1918), Michael Dockery (Jan. 1921)

VOC   Mick Dockery, Seamus Ryan (Jan. 1921), Patrick Callaghan
    (Mar 1921)

Adj   Andy Nevin, Jack Glancy (Jan. 1921), Michael Duignan

QM   Martin Killalea, Pat Mullooly (Jan 1921), Martin Fallon (Mar 1921)

IO   Patrick J. Delahunty

1st Batt. HQ: Boyle
O/C James Feely, Pat Brennan (Mar. 1921)
Area: Boyle, Doon, Ballynameen, Breedogue, Frenchpark, Fairymount

2nd Batt. HQ: Elphin
O/C Seán Owens
Area: Aughrin, Creene, Elphin, Killina, Mantua, Tulsk

3rd Batt. HQ: Strokestown
O/C Bill Doherty
Area: Carniska, Cloonfree, Curraghroe, Kilglass, Kiltrustan, Ruskey,
        Scramogue, Slatta, Strokestown

4th Batt. HQ: Cross
O/C John J. Doyle, Tom Moran, Jimmie O'Brien
Area: Arigna, Ballyfornon, Cootehill, Crossna, Keadue

5th Batt. (new) HQ: Carrick-on-Shannon
O/C Joe McCormack, Jim Dorr, Darby Meehan
Area: Cootehill (switched), Croghan, Drumlion, Drumboylan, Kilmore

Roscommon IRA local military actions referenced in this memoir

2 Oct. 1920	Attack on Frenchpark Barracks
27 Nov. 1920	Attack on Castlenode House, William Walpole's estate
1 Nov. 1920	British raids for IRA throughout Ireland
13 Dec. 1920	Attack on Elphin Dispensary
5 Jan. 1921	Attack on Elphin Barracks; attempt on Frenchpark; engagement near Strokestown Park House; attack on Tarmonbarry Barracks
11 Feb. 1921	Attack on Elphin Barracks

APPENDIX II

Biographical Notes on Significant Local Participants

BEIRNE (OR BYRNE), JOE (1890s–1921): born in Currycramp, Bornacoola, Co. Leitrim; clerk in the Ballinamore railroad station; joined the Irish Volunteers; by January 1921, was Adjutant to the South Leitrim Brigade; selected by Seán Connolly for the Leitrim Flying Column and was in his section in the fight at Selton Hill on 11 March 1921 when killed in action.

BRADY, JAMES J. (c. 1896–1957): born in Gaigue, near Ballinamuck, Co. Longford; as a commercial traveller was a driver with access to a car, thus giving him the opportunity to travel easily; joined the Irish Volunteers; director of elections for Joe McGuinness in his successful election in May 1917; elected to the Longford County Council in 1920; member of the Sinn Féin North Longford District Court created by the Dáil; Secretary of the Ballinamuck Sinn Féin branch; O/C 5th Battalion, Longford Brigade in 1920–1 and participated in the attacks on Ballinamuck Barracks and Top Barracks; on the train from Dublin when Seán MacEoin was arrested; went Anti-Treaty in the Civil War; eventually emigrated to New York; cousin of Tom Brady and Paddy Lynch, both also members of the Longford Flying Column.

CONWAY, SEAMUS (1901–76): born in Lislea, Ballinalee, Co. Longford; joined the Irish Volunteers in spring 1917; in September 1920 was in the Ballinalee Company, 1st Battalion, Longford Brigade; participated in the attacks on Ballymahon Barracks and Arvagh; Vice-O/C and took over the Longford Lying Column after Seán MacEoin's arrest in March 1921;

went Pro-Treaty in the Civil War. See BMH Statement ws443; EOM Military Notebooks UCDA P17b/121, 131, 133; Marie Coleman, *County Longford and the Irish Revolution* (Dublin: Irish Academic Press, 2003).

DAVIS, FRANK/FRANCIS (1897–1979): born near Ballinamuck, Co. Longford; a farmer but able to drive and had access to a car, thus giving him the opportunity to travel easily; joined the Irish Volunteers in 1914, but after the split in 1915, his local unit went inactive; lieutenant in Ballinamuck Company in 1919; sworn into the IRB in April 1919; known to the RIC and being looked for in early 1920; in the reorganisation after September 1920 became quartermaster to the Ballinamuck Company, 1st Battalion, Longford Brigade; on 31 October 1920 shot the newly appointed RIC District Inspector for Granard, Philip St John Kelleher in the Greville Arms Hotel, Granard, shortly after the death of Terence MacSwiney of Cork, and on 1 November shot RIC Constable Cooney; participated in the attacks on Ballinamuck and Ballymahon Barracks; sent by Seán Connolly to reconnoitre the South Leitrim Brigade area in early 1921 and was known there as 'Savage'; joined the North Longford Flying Column as quartermaster; Pro-Treaty in the Civil War. See BMH Statement ws496; EOM Military Notebooks UCDA P17b/121, 131.

DEVINS, SEAMUS (Sligo): joined the Irish Volunteers; became Commandant of the Sligo Brigade; fought occasionally with the Arigna Flying Column in North Roscommon; arrested, sentenced and imprisoned in Dartmoor, England in 1921; Anti-Treaty in the Civil War; killed in action on Ben Bulben Mountain, Co. Donegal, on 20 September 1922. See Katherine Hegarty Thorne, *They Put the Flag a-Flyin': The Roscommon Volunteers, 1916–1923* (Oregon, 2005), p. 468.

DEVITT, MARTIN (MAURTEEN) (Clare): joined the Irish Volunteers, and was VOC Mid-Clare Brigade when Ernie O'Malley first encountered him in March 1919 when O'Malley had been sent down from GHQ to help restructure the brigades in Co. Clare; killed in action at Cahersherkin, Ennistymon, Co. Clare on 24 February 1920. See Ernie O'Malley, *On Another Man's Wound* (Dublin: Anvil Books 2002); O'Farrell, *Who's Who*, p. 165.

DOCKERY, MICHAEL (MICK): born in Drumlish, Drummullin, near Elphin, Co. Roscommon; joined the Irish Volunteers; had known Ernie O'Malley in 1918 when O'Malley was sent down by GHQ to organise North and South Roscommon; participated in a failed attempt on the Carrick-on-Shannon railway station in 1918; in September 1920 was V OC of the North Roscommon Brigade and in January 1921 was elected O/C; participated in the attack on Elphin Barracks in February 1921; arrested in March 1921 after raiding the Boyle Post Office; went Anti-Treaty in the Civil War.

(O') DOHERTY, BILL (WILLIAM/LIAM): born in Dungloe, Co. Donegal; owned a shop in Elphin, Co. Roscommon; joined the Irish Volunteers in 1917; helped in the defence of Ballinalee in 1918; arrested later in 1918 and imprisoned in Sligo Jail; in September 1920 was O/C of the Strokestown Company and the 3rd Battalion of the North Roscommon Brigade; able to drive a car; participated in the attempt to raid Castlenode, near Strokestown to get William Walpole's car; participated in the attack on Elphin Barracks in February 1921, but was arrested later that month; went Anti-Treaty in the Civil War. See EOM Military Notebooks UCDA P17b/131.

FITZGERALD, MICK (Fermoy, Cork): employed as a mill worker in Clondulane; Secretary of the Clondulane Branch of the Irish Transport and General Workers' Union; joined the Irish Volunteers in mid-1917; went on the run due to his activities in the Anti-Conscription Campaign of 1918; a member of the Fermoy Company and became its O/C, 1st Battalion, Cork No. 2 Brigade and Cork No. 2 Brigade Flying Column; participated in the Mallow–Fermoy train hold-up in 1918 and on the attack on Araglen Barracks on 20 April 1919; arrested and then released in 1919; participated in the attack outside Fermoy Wesleyan church in September 1919 and arrested thereafter; by the time of his trial in June 1920, the Cork jurors refused to be impanelled and thus caused a civic crisis; in the meantime Liam Lynch had captured Brigadier General Cuthbert H. T. Lucas and treated him as a prisoner of war, until he escaped; went on hunger strike in Cork Jail and died 67 days later on

17 October 1920, just eight days before Cork Lord Mayor Terence MacSwiney, who also died on hunger strike. See Padraic O'Farrell, *Who's Who in the Irish War of Independence, 1916–1921* (Cork: Mercier, 1980), p. 166.

FLYNN, CHARLIE: born in Co. Leitrim; was the local schoolteacher in Selton Hill village on the day of the attack there; nine of Seán Connolly's men were in his house when he went out to see if the road was clear of British troops, but was apprehended by the RIC District Inspector Gore-Hickman and marched back to his own house at gunpoint; arrested, brought to Carrick-on-Shannon Barracks and charged with conspiracy by withholding names. See EOM Military Notebooks UCDA P17b/132.

KEOGH, TOM (Dublin): joined the Irish Volunteers; involved in manufacture of munitions; participated in the Ashtown ambush on 19 December 1919; drove the horse-drawn mail car in the Castle Mail Raid of 1919; a member of 'the Squad' starting in 1920 and shot two Auxiliaries on Bloody Sunday morning; participated in and was captured after the burning of the Dublin Custom House, May 1921. See O'Farrell, *Who's Who*, pp. 82–3.

KIELY, JERRY (Tipperary): joined the Irish Volunteers and then the IRA and was a member of the 4th Battalion, Third Tipperary Brigade; assisted Ernie O'Malley in his organising activities in Co. Tipperary and subsequently when fighting with the 2nd Southern Division; Anti-Treaty in the Civil War; killed in action in early April 1923. See O'Malley, *On Another Man's Wound*; UCDA P106/754 (1–2); Dan Breen, *My Fight for Irish Freedom* (Dublin: Anvil, 1989); John R. Shelley, *A Short History of the 3rd Tipperary Brigade* (1966).

MACEOIN, SEÁN (1893–1973): born in Ballinlough, near Ballinalee, Co. Longford; a blacksmith following in a long line of blacksmiths; became member of the IRB in 1914 in Granard; joined Clonbroney Irish National Volunteers in 1914; was not mobilised on Easter Sunday 1916; served successively as section commander, lieutenant, company captain and O/C 1st Battalion of the Longford Brigade, 1917–21; VOC and Director of Operations of Longford Brigade, 1920–1; formed a County Circle for IRB in 1917, later a member of Provincial Centre and eventually a member of the Supreme Council; involved in engagements in Ballinalee, November 1920, at Martins' cottage, Ballinalee, 7–8 January 1921 and Clonfin ambush, 2 February 1921; arrested at Mullingar Station, 2 March 1921 and sentenced to death for the murder of District Inspector Thomas McGrath at Martins' cottage; released following an ultimatum from Michael Collins prior to commencement of Dáil debate on entering into talks with Britain prior to Truce; went Pro-Treaty in the Civil War and had a long career in national politics. See BMH Statement WS 1716; Seán MacEoin Papers, UCDA; Padraic O'Farrell, *The Blacksmith of Ballinalee: Seán MacEoin* (Mullingar, 1993); *Longford Leader*.

MCGUINNESS, JOE (1875–1922): born near Tarmonbarry, Co. Roscommon; a draper and became involved in Gaelic League; went to Dublin and joined the Irish Volunteers there at their inception; had been a lieutenant in "C" Company, 1st Dublin Battalion, Dublin Brigade, and was involved in 1916; when arrested, he was convicted and assigned to Lewes Prison in England; in April 1917 while still in prison, he was nominated as the Sinn Féin candidate to oppose the Irish Parliamentary Party candidate, Paddy McKenna, in the Longford by-election to be held on 9 May 1917; his older brother, Frank McGuinness, had a shop in Longford; won the election by 37 votes; arrested and imprisoned again in 1918 and 1921, and re-elected during each jail term; member of the standing committee of the Sinn Féin Executive, 1918–22, director of elections for Sinn Féin, 1919; director of publicity for Dáil, September–November, 1919, during Ernest Blythe's imprisonment; went Pro-Treaty but died in May 1922 prior to outbreak of Civil War. See Coleman, *County Longford*.

MULLOOLY, PAT (1894–1977): born near Luggs, Kiltrustan, Strokestown, Co. Roscommon; a railroad worker; joined the Irish Volunteers in 1914 but was inactive until 1917; responded to an advertisement placed by Michael Collins seeking people to activate the Irish Volunteers locally; became captain of the Kiltrustan Volunteers; had known Ernie O'Malley in 1918 when O'Malley had been sent down by GHQ to organise North and South Roscommon; had participated in a failed attempt on the Carrick-on-Shannon railway station in 1918; moved to Dublin, while working for the railroad; joined the IRB while in Dublin; ordered back to North Roscommon as Brigade quartermaster; arrested and held overnight in Dublin Castle in Dublin in December 1920 at which time he met O'Malley again and when released the following day was able to report to Michael Collins as to O'Malley's location; elected Adjutant of the North Roscommon Brigade in January 1921; went Pro-Treaty and joined the National Army during the Civil War. See BMH Statements ws 955, 1086, 1087; EOM Military Notebooks UCDA P17b/131, 132, 136; Kathleen Hegarty Thorne, *They Put the Flag a-Flyin': The Roscommon Volunteers, 1916–1923* (Oregon, 2005), pp. 392–3.

MURPHY, MICHAEL/MICK (1899–1968): born in Briskill, near Newtownforbes, Co. Longford; joined the Irish Volunteers in Briskill Company, 2nd Battalion, Longford Brigade; joined the IRB in 1919; remained in the Briskill Company upon transfer to the IRA in 1919; O/C 2nd Battalion, Longford Brigade, 1920–1; had been sent in 1920 into Leitrim as part of the IRA Republican Police by Seán Connolly to look for illicit whiskey stills; participated in attack on Drumlish Barracks and the attempt on Edgeworthstown Barracks; went Pro-Treaty in the Civil War and served as a commandant in the Free State army. See BMH Statement ws479; EOM Military Notebooks UCDA P17b/131.

O'REILLY, CAPT. JOHN JOSEPH (1900–21): born in Derrinkeher McDonald, Aughnasheelin, Co. Leitrim; joined the Irish Volunteers; captain of the Aughnasheelin Company, 3rd Battalion of the South Leitrim Brigade in 1920; attended meetings with Seán Connolly in Longford in September 1920, and participated in attack on the Arvagh Barracks immediately thereafter; quartermaster to the South Leitrim Brigade in January 1921; selected by Seán Connolly for the Leitrim Flying Column and was in his section in the fight at Selton Hill on 11 March 1921 where he was wounded in action while trying to throw a grenade and died later that day.

RYAN-LACKEN, PADDY (Tipperary): joined the Irish Volunteers and active in his Tipperary area; killed in action at Knockfine, Co. Tipperary on 6 June 1921. See O'Farrell, *Who's Who*, p.174.

SWEENEY, BERNIE/BERNARD: born in Tullyhusker, Ballinamore, Co. Leitrim; joined the Irish Volunteers in Ballinamore in 1917 that later became the Ballinamore Company of which he was company captain, 1st Battalion of the South Leitrim Brigade in the November 1920 reorganisation; joined the IRB in the meantime; was selected by Seán Connolly for the Leitrim Flying Column and was in his section in the fight at Selton Hill on 11 March 1921 where though wounded, managed to hide in a deep ditch and escape from the area that night; his wounds were attended to by Dr D. P. Dolan, the Brigade Medical Officer; was sheltered in the Quills' house higher up the mountains and then kept in Red Burke's house to convalesce; was able to rejoin the flying column in May 1921. See BMH Statement WS 1194; EOM Military Notebooks UCDA P17b/132.

TRAYNOR, THOMAS (Tullow, Co Carlow): married with seven children; joined the Irish Volunteers and was an officer in the IRA; involved in shooting of an Auxiliary at Brunswick Street (now Pearse Street), and was arrested and beaten by the 'Igoe Gang', then tried, found guilty, held in Mountjoy Jail, Dublin, and sentenced to death; meanwhile the South Tipperary Brigade on 23 April 1921 captured RIC District Inspector Gilbert N. Potter, and made an unsuccessful attempt to exchange Potter's life for Traynor's; Traynor was executed on 15 April 1921 and Potter was executed on 27 April. See O'Farrell, *Who's Who*, p. 175.

WALL, SEÁN (Bruff, East Limerick): son of small landowner, became successful building contractor specialising in creameries and owned a steam and threshing mill that had introduced mechanical milking to Limerick; joined the Irish Volunteers; participated in the attack on Kilmallock RIC Barracks in May 1920; elected Chairman of the Limerick County Council on 25 June 1920, while still Commandant of the East Limerick Brigade, thus illustrating the complementary nature of the political and military wings of the independence movement; active in the

Dáil Courts; killed in action in Limerick on 16 May 1921. See O'Farrell, *Who's Who*, p. 175.

WRYNN, SEAMUS (1897–1921): born in Drumcromman, Ballinamore, Co. Leitrim; joined the Irish Volunteers; captain of the Aughnasheelin Company, 3rd Battalion of the South Leitrim Brigade in 1920; attended meetings with Seán Connolly in Longford in September 1920, and participated in attack on the Arvagh Barracks immediately thereafter; was quartermaster to the South Leitrim Brigade in January 1921; selected by Seán Connolly for the Leitrim Flying Column and was in his section in the fight at Selton Hill on 11 March 1921 where he was wounded in action while trying to throw a grenade and died later that day.

APPENDIX III

Connolly Family Tree

Andrew Connolly m. Sarah McDowell
(1800–85)   (d. 1883)

John m. Margaret Corcoran
(1860–1936)   (18?–19??)

Gerald (188?–188?)

Seán (1890–1921)

Thomas (1894–1964)

Patrick (1895–1935)

Louis (1903–23)

Mary (Maura) Josephine (1900–66) m. Seán MacLochlainn

Sarah (1904–50) m. Mr McNamee

Una (1927–27)

Pearse (1928–2002)

Donald (Donal) (1934–) m. Rita McGranaghan

Lorna (1937–) m. Seamus Delaney

Enda MacLochlainn/McLaughlin (1925–2001) m. Terry Young

David   Stephen   Alona   Susan

Suzanne   John

Barry   Anna   Caroline

John James (1917–80)

Kevin   Elizabeth m. G. Gray

Marie m. H. Drumm

Notes

Introduction

1   See pp. 15–16, 47, 73, 105–11, 167.

2   Ernie O'Malley, *On Another Man's Wound* (London: Rich & Cowan, 1936 and most recently Anvil Books, 2002). This book covers up to the Truce of 12 July 1921.

3   Ernie O'Malley, *The Singing Flame,* ed. Frances-Mary Blake (Dublin: Anvil Books, 1979). This book covers the period from the Truce though his release from internment in July 1924.

4   For a full history of the efforts see Gerard O'Brien, *Irish Governments and the Guardianship of Historical Records, 1922–72* (Dublin, Four Courts, 2004).

5   The Bureau of Military History Statements are available as copies in the National Archives of Ireland and the originals are available, by appointment, at the Bureau of Military History, Cathal Brugha Barracks, Rathmines, Dublin 6.

6   The Ernie O'Malley Papers at UCD Archives are divided into two categories: UCDA P17a/-for papers and UCDA P17b/- for Military Notebooks covering the First and Second Series on interviews. They are all on microfilm and a complete index has been prepared.

7   See p. 18 below.

8   Ernie O'Malley, *Raids and Rallies*, ed. Frances-Mary Blake (Dublin: Anvil Books, 1982).

9   Padraic O'Farrell, *The Ernie O'Malley Story* (Cork: Mercier, 1984).

10   Richard English and Cormac O'Malley (eds), *Prisoners: The Civil War Letters of Ernie O'Malley* (Dublin: Poolbeg, 1991). This book included only 48 communications from the period of his incarceration from November 1922 to July 1924.

11 Richard English, *Ernie O'Malley: IRA Intellectual* (Oxford: Clarendon Press, 1996).

12 Cormac O'Malley and Anne Dolan (eds), *No Surrender Here: The Civil War Papers of Ernie O'Malley, 1921–1924* (forthcoming, Dublin: Lilliput).

13 Katherine Hegarty Thorne, *They Put the Flag a-Flyin': The Roscommon Volunteers, 1916–1923* (Oregon, 2005).

14 English and O'Malley (eds), *Prisoners*, no. 30, p. 69; no. 33, p. 97; and no. 30, p.106.

Chapter 1 Longford

1 Richard Robert Madden, *Antrim and Down in '98* (London: Burnes, Oates & Washbourne [1860?]); John Mitchel, *The History of Ireland, Ancient and Modern* (1st edn, New York: D. & J. Sadleir, 1868); Mitchel's *Jail Journal or Five Years in British Prisons* (1st edn [1854]); A. M. Sullivan, *New Ireland* (London, 1877); T. D., A.M. and D. B. Sullivan, *Speeches from the Dock or Protests of Irish Patriotism*, ed. Seán Ua Ceallaigh, 1953 edn (Dublin: Gill).

2 Sullivan et al., *Speeches from the Dock*, p. 230.

3 Sir John Perrott (1527–92), Lord Deputy of Ireland, Sir Richard Bingham (1528–99), Governor of Connaught, and Sir Conyers Clifford (d.1599) were three senior Representatives in Ireland under the rule of the English Queen Elizabeth I.

4 After efforts were made by many people from a variety of sources, the list of unknown men has been documented, see Appendix II.

5 For the family tree of Seán Connolly's family, see p. 184.

6 The Depot in the Phoenix Park, Dublin, was the training college for RIC candidates.

7 There was also a Land War incident in 1881 in Drumlish, which was only six miles from Ballinalee, and these incidents often had rippling effects on their surrounding communities.

8 In 1914 after the passage of the Home Rule Act, John Redmond had urged the Irish National Volunteers to serve in the British forces during the Great War of 1914–1918, and about 90 per cent followed his urging and decimated the Volunteers.

9 The Irish National Foresters, known as the Foresters, were a friendly, fraternal organisation with a nationalist ethos. At its height they had branches all over Ireland and even went overseas with the Irish emigrants.

Chapter 2 Longford, 1916–18

1 The South Longford by-election took place on 9 May 1918 and was won by Joseph McGuinness, then a prisoner in Lewes Prison, Lewes, East Sussex, England.

2 Several British army Lancer cavalry units were based in Ireland. It is possible that the 5th Royal Irish Lancers, based in the Curragh, were involved in Dublin in Easter Week while the 9th Queen's Royal Lancers were deployed in the Leitrim, Longford, Roscommon area. See http://www.armymuseums. org.uk/sot-cavalry.htm and http://myhome.ispdr.net.au/~mgrogan/cork/ regiment.htm

3 The Tithe War of 1831–6 refers to the Catholic opposition to the payment of tithes to maintain the Church of Ireland. After considerable local bloodshed a Tithe Commutation Act was passed in 1839, but the disestablishment of the Church of Ireland did not happen until 1869.

4 The term 'separation women' referred to those women whose husbands were off on British army active duty and thus their family at home was living separately from them.

5 The Anti-Conscription Pledge to resist any law which might be passed requiring conscription in Ireland was taken after Mass on Sunday 21 April 1918 throughout Ireland.

Chapter 3 Longford and National Developments, 1918–20

1 For Battalion areas within Longford Brigade, see p. 14, 173–4.

2 The IRB organisational structure was founded on the small active cell concept and included a local centre with probably several local centres in each county, a county centre, a provincial centre and a supreme council. Many of the leading local leaders were inducted into the IRB which had its own command structure independent of – though partially overlapping with – the Irish Volunteers and later the IRA. Seán Connolly was a member of the IRB.

3 The Nine Years War was from 1594 to 1603.

4 A rising out is an old Irish expression referring to an old Gaelic arrangement when local kings or chieftains did not have standing armies and hence they would require their tenants or sub-chieftains to supply them with warriors for a particular cause; such a demand for the supply of arms was referred to as a rising out. In later years it referred more to a popular physical force rising of an insurgent force against the dominating British imperial forces. See also p. 61.

5   In the parliamentary elections held in Ireland on 14 December 1918, the Irish Parliamentary Party won seats only in Armagh, Belfast Falls Road, Donegal East, Down South, Tyrone Northeast and Waterford City. They also won one seat in Liverpool.

Chapter 4 Longford, 1920

1   Very lights were commonly used in military operations to light up the sky at night so that the military could observe any suspicious movement or object. They were shot from a Very light pistol using heavy cartridges. See their use in military operations, pp. 65, 73, 102.

2   Geordie is a common reference to a man from Tyneside in the north-east of England. Geordie is, however, referred to as having a Yorkshire voice later in the narrative.

Chapter 5 Longford, September 1920

1   Uncle Toby was uncle to Tristram Shandy, about whom Laurence Sterne (1713–68) wrote his novel, *The Life and Opinions of Tristram Shandy, Gentleman*, which was first published in nine volumes from 1759 to 1767. Uncle Toby was known for his retelling of military strategies.

Chapter 7 North Roscommon, November–December, 1920

1   Philip St John Howlett Kelleher: see Jim Herlihy, *The Royal Irish Constabulary Officers: A Biographical Dictionary and Genealogical Guide: 1816–1922* (Dublin: Four Courts, 2005), p. 184.

2   The first chapter of *The Tain* is entitled 'The Pillow Talk' as it refers to the discussion between Ailill and Medb in the royal bed at their fort in Crughan, Co. Roscommon, when they were resting on their pillows and started to boast to each other, which boasting ultimately resulted in the invasion of Ulster by Ailill and his army. See *The Tain* published by Dolmen Press and Oxford University Press, 1970, p. 52.

3   Samhain is the Irish for November, and it also refers to the pagan festival of Samhain, which was celebrated annually on 1 November and that festival date has been incorporated into the Christian calendar as All Saints' Day and is followed by All Souls' Day.

Chapter 8 Dublin Castle, December 1920

1   When Ernie O'Malley was captured in Inistioge, Co. Kilkenny in early December 1920, he was brought to Woodstock House which was the local headquarters for the Auxiliaries. He identified himself only as Bernard Stewart and gave no other information. Soon he was transferred to Dublin Castle where he was put through a more rigorous and torturous examination which he fully described in *On Another Man's Wound*. Thus he happened to be incarcerated in Dublin Castle when Pat Mullooly and Mick O'Connell were arrested and also placed there.

2   Major King and Captain J. L. Hardy were the two British officers who were involved in torturing Ernie O'Malley in Dublin Castle. Their names, and indeed the entire torture segment, were not included in the original 1936 edition of *On Another Man's Wound* for legal reasons, but they have been included in more recent editions.

3   Mick O'Connell's name was identified in Statement WS1086, p. 26, made by Patrick Mullooly to the BMH, dated 3 June 1954.

Chapter 9 Roscommon: October 1920–February 1921

1   Conor Clune, who is referred to on p. 110 above as having been bayoneted and shot in November 1920, was the nephew of Dr Patrick Joseph Clune, Archbishop of Perth.

Chapter 10 Leitrim: January–April 1921

1   The East Yorks referred to the East Yorkshire Regiment in the British army.

2   Ernie O'Malley notes that there were three battalions in the South Leitrim Brigade in the period January–March 1921. During the Civil War there were also apparently Anti-Treaty 4th and 5th Battalions. For the structure of the South Leitrim Brigade, see pp. 171–2.

3   The South Leitrim Flying Column was divided into two sections in early March 1921 by Seán Connolly as follows: the first section was led by Seán Connolly and included Michael Baxter, Joe Beirne, Paddy Guckian, Jack Hunt, P. J. McDermott, Frank McKeown, Andy McPartland, Captain John Joe O'Reilly, John Joe O'Reilly, Bernie Sweeney, and Seamus Wrynn; the second section was

led by Seán Mitchell and included Mattie Boylan, Michael Geoghegan, Michael Martin, Harry McKeon, Joe Nagle, and Tom O'Reilly.

4   Thomas O'Brien Gore-Hickman (1892–1982), the RIC District Inspector in Mohill, was from Co. Clare. After the Selton Hill incident, he immediately left for England and did not return until after the Truce. He emigrated thereafter to Alberta, Canada. See Jim Herlihy, *The Royal Irish Constabulary Officers: A Biographical Dictionary and Genealogical Guide: 1816–1922* (Dublin: Four Courts, 2005), p. 145.

5   Dr Patrick J. Dolan was in fact the South Leitrim Brigade Medical Officer.

6   The two men were Paddy Guckian and P. J. McDermott, according to the radio lecture by Matty Fox Senior on Shannonside Radio on the subject of Selton Hill, a CD copy of which was provided by Donal MacLochlainn, nephew of Seán Connolly.

7   According to the BMH Statement WS1263 of Charles Pinkman, dated 5 October 1955, pp. 12–13, 'it would seem as if Connolly was in the act of throwing a grenade when he was hit by an enemy bullet. He fell where he was and the grenade, from which the pin had been withdrawn, exploded beside or underneath his body.' That explains how Connolly had been so severely wounded. Pinkman was the Intelligence Officer for the South Leitrim Brigade and had been asked to make an official report on the incident of Selton Hill. Moreover, according to a local Ballinalee historian, Matty Fox, when Connolly's body lay in the Longford Cathedral sawdust had to be spread under the coffin to absorb the dripping blood which suggests that the wounds had indeed been extensive. Matty Fox was from Ballinalee, was distantly related to the Connolly family, had lived near them in France, and had worked on the Connolly farm for some years in the 1930s. Later he left to become a postman.

8   The Bedford and Hampshire Regiment officer killed in the Sheemore ambush a week previous was Lt Wilson, see p. 151.

9   Matty Fox in his radio interview identified the priest as Fr Dalton.

10   According to Matty Fox's radio interview, no one would officially identify Seán Connolly's body. However, his brother, Tommy Connolly, went to Carrick-on-Shannon to bring his body home to Longford. Since his body had been dragged through the fields at the time of his capture, it was covered in mud and manure; his body was washed by the McGuinness sisters of Main Street, Longford, before it was returned to the family for services in Longford Cathedral.

11   In Pinkman's BMH Statement, he reports that William Latimer was going to attend to the preparation for his mother, who had died the previous day, and encountered Dr Pentland on the road, and that is probably when he passed

along the information as to the location of the IRA flying column. Dr Pentland in turn passed along the information to RIC Inspector Gore-Hickman (ibid.). In his radio interview Matty Fox noted that Latimer's mother had died only that morning.

12 Pinkman gives a detailed description of this incident including several grenades being thrown into the house, Latimer's surrender, and subsequent execution (ibid.).

13 Pinkman notes that Pentland died by a truck hitting him while standing on the pavement about three years later in the London area to which he had been traced (ibid.).

14 In addition to those commemorations mentioned in the original version of this memoir, there are now several other reminders of Seán Connolly in Longford including the Republican Plot in the Clonbroney Chapel Cemetery, which includes his name in Irish as Seán Ó Congaile, and the stained glass window in his honour in the Ballinalee Church.

Index

Ailill, *Tain* 96

America *see* United States

American pressure 44

Ancient Order of Hibernians 23, 31, 32

An Dáil *see* Dáil Éireann

Anglo-Irish 50

An tOglach, Sinn Féin official
    publication 53, 55

Araglin Barracks (Co. Cork) 1920 56

Ardagh (Co. Longford) 62

Ardagullion Bog (Co. Roscommon) 102

Armistice, November 1918 46

art 110

artists (Italian): Botticelli, Piero della
    Francesca, Masaccio, Monaco
    110

Arvagh Barracks (Co. Cavan) 74, 75, 131

Ashe, Thomas, Ballinalee 35

Athlone (Co. Westmeath) 33, 70

Athlone Printing Works, Athlone 33

Attymus (Co. Leitrim) 153–54

Aughnacliffe (Co. Leitrim) 75, 81

Aughnasheelin (Co. Leitrim) 131, 134

Australia 113

Auxiliary/Auxiliaries 4, 80, 86–7, 95–7,
    107–8, 110, 115, 117, 120–1, 127,
    133, 137, 140, 143–4, 146

Bachelor's Walk (Dublin) 38

bail, position against taking 39

Ballagh (Co. Roscommon) 89, 92

Ballinalee (Co. Longford) 18–19, 20–2,
    25, 31, 35, 60, 75, 81, 94–5,
    101–3, 125, 133, 164, 167

Ballinalee Barracks (Co. Longford) 94, 102

Ballinameen (Co. Roscommon) 95, 97,
    113, 119–20, 122

Ballinamore (Co. Leitrim) 74–5, 136–47,
    139, 153, 156, 161, 166

Ballinamore parish (Co. Roscommon)
    85–6

Ballinamuck (Co. Longford) 21, 26,
    63–4, 66, 78–9, 167

Ballinasloe (Co. Roscommon) 107

Ballyduff (Co. Leitrim) 161

Ballymahon/Barracks (Co. Longford)
    33–4, 70–2, 75

Ballyroddy School (Co. Leitrim) 127

Bandra (Co. Longford) 65

Banna Strand (Co. Kerry) 99

Barnes, George (London) 44

Barry (Co. Longford) 71

Baxter, Michael (Co. Leitrim) Flying
    Column 131, 153, 159, 160, 162,
    169

Beasley/Béaslaí, Piaras GHQ Dublin 95

Bedford and Hampshire Regiment,
    British Army, Boyle (Co.
    Roscommon) 151, 158, 163

Beirne, Joe (Joseph) (Co. Leitrim) Adj
    Leitrim Bde, Flying Column
    131, 156, 159, 160, 162, 169, 176